You Couldn't
Make It Up

Also by Jeremy Kyle

I'm Only Being Honest

Jeremy
KYLE

You Couldn't
Make It Up

HODDER &
STOUGHTON

First published in Great Britain in 2010 by Hodder & Stoughton
An Hachette UK company

1

Copyright © Jeremy Kyle 2010

The right of Jeremy Kyle to be identified as the Author
of the Work has been asserted by him in accordance with the
Copyright, Designs and Patents Act 1988.

Some names and identities have been changed
to protect the privacy of the individuals involved.

A CIP catalogue record for this title is available from the British Library

Hardback ISBN 978 1 444 70405 1
Trade Paperback ISBN 978 1 444 70519 5

Typeset in Plantin Light by Ellipsis Books Limited, Glasgow

Printed and bound by CPI Mackays, Chatham ME5 8TD

Hodder & Stoughton policy is to use papers that are natural, renewable
and recyclable products and made from wood grown in sustainable forests.
The logging and manufacturing processes are expected to conform to
the environmental regulations of the country of origin.

Hodder & Stoughton Ltd
338 Euston Road
London NW1 3BH

www.hodder.co.uk

To my four beautiful children,
Hattie, Alice, Ava and Henry.
This one's for you. x

Contents

Contents

Before We Start . . .

There are some things in life you expect to achieve, there are others you might merely one day hope to. Beyond all those are the surprises, good and bad, that explode without warning into your life.

As I steadily built a career that spanned recruitment, sales, radio and then TV, I always had at least one eye on the next rung of the ladder. I wanted to be the best I could in any job I was doing but I knew that, sooner or later, the temptation to challenge myself in uncharted waters would always get the better of me. Curiosity as to whether or not I could cut it with the bigger boys has fed my ambition and fuelled my drive for as long as I can remember. I never imagined even for a second that my time in recruitment might lead to a job in television but even back then I knew my talents as a recruiter might serve me well in advertising sales – the next, and better paid, step up. My sales career took me to a radio station and that led to an unexpected opportunity to present a show. After nearly a decade in radio, I hoped beyond hope that I might get a crack at television and over the past year or so I have wondered what it might be like to take what I do here and see if it could work in America.

I

I am blessed that these things happened and are still happening to me and I focused hard on making the best of what I had whilst waiting for the chance to test myself on another level. And so, while I never planned for the prize to be a job in television, the hard work done and the little battles won, week to week, wherever I have been, have seen the succession of doors opening that led me to this point. I have to tell you though, one thing I never reckoned on doing, no matter where I was in my career, was sitting down to write a book. And yet here I am welcoming you to my second!

I'll start by thanking you for buying this copy. If you have borrowed it from a friend or even been sent one for free I'll thank you for taking the time to read it. You might be stealing bread from the mouths of my children but at least you are here to share in what has become something of a mini labour of love for me.

I don't claim that this will be the most spectacular read of your lives. I am no Shakespeare, this is no Pulitzer Prize winner and I doubt it will be troubling any shortlists for the serious literary prizes. But, hopefully, that is no reason for it not to be as enjoyable to read as it was to write. I never expected to get one bite at the book-writing cherry, so to have now had two is something very special, and very exciting.

I have tried to pack it with all the opinions and ideas that have stabbed away at my conscience over the past eighteen months. It has also been an opportunity to reflect a little more on the way my family life informs all those opinions and ideas.

When I was writing my first book I was largely trying to answer the questions that had been put to me over the years since launching *The Jeremy Kyle Show*. I hadn't really given too many interviews back then so *I'm Only Being Honest* was a great platform to speak about my show, the issues we cover, the sorts of guests I tend to meet, the problems they face and what personal experience I'd had of confronting my own demons and past mistakes. It was a serious book about serious topics and I tried to write it seriously. Hopefully, readers of that book, whether they agreed with me or not, would at least acknowledge that I tried to treat the subjects I was writing about with the respect they deserved. I described things as I saw them based on personal experience and really was trying only to be honest.

The scope of this book was always going to be different. As a result it should feel a bit different to read. Anyone who was expecting more of the same this time round – I'm sorry, you may be disappointed. I haven't changed, my views are largely the same and everything I wrote back then I would still stand by today. However, people have grown so familiar with the show that it now seems their attention has turned to what they can learn about me as a person. The questions I get asked these days are not always all about the show in the way they once were. Increasingly, conversations involve some digging to find the 'real me', to see what I'm really like off camera.

Some people want to know if I am always as angry in 'real life' as they perceive me to be on TV. Others only want to know about what it's actually like to be on TV and how the industry works. With increasing frequency I find I am fielding questions about how I first got the job, what I do differently now I'm in the job and what it is like to be a so-called celebrity. People seem curious as to whether I've 'changed' in the last five years. They want to know whether I run around ranting at star-studded parties, if I've ever got into fights with those in the media who've slagged me off and, basically, if I've disappeared up my own arse! In the first book I tried to answer all the questions that were being pumped at me about the show, in this one I'll attempt to answer most of what's asked about the life I lead when I'm not filming it.

When I wrote *I'm Only Being Honest* I was still finding my feet as someone who made a living in the media spotlight. I have grown a lot since then and am now more comfortable in my 'celebrity' skin. I have been to a few parties and made a few friends but I've clearly made some enemies too. This book will detail much of what I've seen since joining the crazy celebrity circus. I'll talk about the lavish perks that come the way of many a celebrity and some of the pitfalls too.

As I have said, I am still the same person. The person you may have seen on TV is very much me; the person you may have read about last time round, that is me too. I am still pretty forthright, I still speak pretty plainly and I'll still try to give an honest answer to all questions put my way. As well as the personal stuff, I wanted to talk about the more ridiculous, hard to believe and downright disgraceful things that are allowed to go on right under our noses. Fat children, terrible parents, soft-touch sentencing and what I'd do with 'Lotto Lout' Michael Carroll will all get the Jeremy Kyle treatment here, as each are at the centre of stories that, really, *You Couldn't Make Up*.

This book, a little like the last, is not without its confessions.

You might be surprised to learn that in the next three hundred pages or so I'll out myself as a food thief and an accidental butcher of domestic pets. I'll tell you about the day I nearly died, the day I really died and detail a battle I once lost with an aggressively inserted suppository.

What you see is what you get with me on the TV show but I don't walk around with a microphone and a set of DNA results when I'm off stage. Perhaps it would be good if I did because it seems that whenever I am not in the safe, secure and structured environment of a TV studio, my life tends to fall apart a little. I have an uncanny knack for putting my foot in it, for attracting disaster at every turn and for crashing through life in a way that would make even Frank Spencer wince.

You Couldn't Make It Up shows a little of what my life outside of work is really like. In the professional arena there are some oddities to explore but they are as nothing compared to the lunacy of life at home in the Kyle family household! At work I stand up to some no-good dads but at home I have to ensure I am up to the job myself. As you will read in these pages, that is not always easy and I frequently cock things up no matter how hard I try.

I am showing and being a bit more 'me' too. Believe it or not, I laugh and joke quite a bit through any given day but because of the job I do, people very rarely get to see that side of me. Many don't even know it exists. The whole process of opening up, of sharing some of the more ludicrous stories that have punctuated my life, has been fascinating for me. I've relaxed and I've laughed as I've taken my walks down my Memory Lane. I've thought and I've raged as I've contemplated the iniquities and the injustices that still plague this country. It has been good to explore and I only hope you share in some of that enjoyment as you read my efforts to accomplish one of those things that never in my wildest dreams did I imagine I would get to do.

I

The Manopause . . .
(Medically Proven Fact:
I *Am* Getting Old)

I knew it. I bloody well knew it! I've said before that the complaint viewers most often level against me is that I *say* I'm an old man when really, at forty-four, I'm not. Surprising that this provokes the most complaints I know, given the many gripes, grievances and ugly accusations used to slate me, but there you go.

Recently I have been wondering whether my basic problem is that meeting so many youngsters with so many issues (drink, drugs, joblessness, all endured, in some cases even enjoyed and frequently passed on to their own kids) has made me feel very old. Many of the people I meet on my show manage to cram in so much destruction, when they're less than half my age. Maybe I'm not an old man after all, perhaps I just feel old before my time when hearing a particularly frustrating or miserable story . . . Wherever the feeling of weariness is coming from, it's a real shame because I always hoped that I might, just might, be a young forty-something. And in many respects, I am. I have everything I ever hoped for – beautiful children, gorgeous young wife, healthy diet and an active lifestyle – I qualify on all counts, so maybe those viewers are right and I have over-egged my age on stage.

Unfortunately, my doctor tells me it's not just that. Despite my healthy diet and my wonderful family, this feeling of ageing is not all in my mind. I am definitely just getting old. Worse, I am beginning to fall apart. Now, I realise that confirmation of this news might plunge the Royal Mail or even the whole economy into crisis but I have to tell the truth. Readers, viewers and complainers all, the thousands you currently spend on stamps and texts each week can now be saved and put to better use. Don't bother continuing with your calls for me to stop carping on about sliding into old age, because my doctor tells me that is *precisely* what is happening. All protests received from now on will be ignored on medical grounds. These days I can't even read the letters without straining my failing eyes but even if I could, there's no longer any point. At forty-four, I might seem a spring chicken to some, but there's no escaping the fact that I've somehow graduated from 'getting on a bit' to the full-blown state of getting old.

My doctor was only really confirming the message that so many of my rapidly decaying senses have been sending me for quite some time. Typically for a man of 'advancing years' I was far too stubborn to acknowledge the mounting evidence provided on a daily basis by my body. It was my knee collapsing beneath me whilst doing nothing more manly and strenuous than getting up from a chair, that eventually forced me to go and talk to a professional. I had to be helped out of the heap I had made of myself in the living room, and then Tubigripped so tightly I lost all the feeling in my toes. I hobbled miserably around the house for a while until my wife, fearing moaning of Man-Flu proportions, bundled me into the car and insisted I go and see a doctor. I did as I was told but I wasn't prepared for the bluntness with which my new condition – getting old – would be diagnosed.

I'll never forget that day. I sat in his offices, thinking that our meeting would be more check-up-and-chat than anything else. After a brief description of my malady the doctor ran through the options.

'Mr Kyle, do you play sport regularly?'

'No.'

'I see, well, do you work out vigorously at the gym?'

'Um, no.'

'In that case, I am afraid to say that you must be getting old.'

And with that, it was confirmed. Brutally. Stress fracture of the right kneecap, painful cyst lurking beneath, no longer young, way past my best and never likely to play a game for West Ham. The dream was over. Bugger. I perked up a bit when I thought that all the questions about sport and fitness and 'vigorous' workouts at the gym might mean I was in for some good news. Maybe he had seen something in the test results that meant I was supremely fit, and in fine working order for a man of my age, right? Wrong! Now, I've never considered donning Speedos and spray-tan for a try-out at Mr Universe but I always thought that, in my own way, I was in pretty good shape: don't drink much, never touched drugs, not fat, eat healthily, have most of my hair left – I thought I might be in line for compliments and gold stars from the doctor, but no. Instead he said he'd recommend me for surgery.

It was the prospect of having this operation, and the time I was told to take off work either side of it, that really forced me to re-evaluate things. There had been evidence of ageing in the past that I had blithely ignored but now it was time to face facts. I was also extremely worried about the operation. I don't mind admitting that I'm scared of needles and I was petrified of being put under anaesthetic. I hate not being in control and I had nightmare visions of everything that might go wrong in the operating theatre. It was all fine in the end, of course but, typically, despite being unconscious throughout, I still managed to talk the whole way through the procedure. I don't remember a thing of what I said but the surgeon said my witterings were quite remarkable, though thankfully not too distracting!

Ultimately the operation was a success and I was told to get back to normal. I'm lucky in that I don't get ill very often and the time I'd been forced to spend resting had given me an opportunity to reflect on just how quickly the last few years had flashed by. The charge was 'getting old', the verdict was 'guilty' and, quite apart from the physical stuff, I had to acknowledge that I had changed.

- Increasing impatience – tick.
- Growing irritability – tick.
- Modern music now resembling 'angry noise' – tick.
- Lifestyle choices of too many youths incomprehensible to me – tick.
- Rigid belief that certain things should return to 'how they were in my day' – tick. Oh dear . . .

Most of these standard changes in attitude I knew were coming, and I fully expect them to become bigger issues as the years tick by to pension and bus pass. They are as understandable as they are inevitable. New generations come through, break away from their immediate predecessors, reinvent themselves for *their* time and stake a claim for an era that they too will look back on all too fondly, especially when their offspring begin to inhabit and shape a world that seems so at odds with the safety and security of their own. I could almost cope with these things, but the actual physical health stuff was driving me mad. I had half-crippled myself getting out of a chair and had been told that my body's newfound fragility was brought on by nothing more sinister than middle age. Feeling suddenly under threat from my own body, I scoured the internet for relevant information. Heart attacks, strokes, liver disease, respiratory failure, even male pattern baldness – I dutifully read about the risks and realities of all of them. But not one website I visited mentioned what is happening to me and to all men my age: the manopause.

I don't know if a manual will ever be written on the male menopause, but I think we need one. My dad found it awkward enough to go into the birds and the bees with me as a child so there wasn't much chance of him explaining all the surprises my body would spring on me as I got older. I'm on my own here.

I've only just come round to accepting that I've probably lived more years than I have left. But it turns out that there are all sorts of other indignities and infirmities I am expected to come to terms with as I crash through mid-life crisis and plough on into old age. I feel conned. For example, when exactly was someone planning to explain to me the perils of ears and noses that will never stop growing? Quite aside from increasing problems with my knees, eyes and bald-spot, my face is besieged on all sides by things that will not stop growing until the day I die! Not long ago a guest on my show berated me for sporting ridiculous 'big, flappy ears.' I have to admit they are bigger than most, so the thought of them continuing their quest to take over my head is really quite frightening. I can't pick up satellite signals with my 'dishes' and no birds have yet attempted to nest in them, but the knowledge that they are big and getting bigger all the time is not welcome. Take one look at Wogan's lugs and you might have some idea of what lies in store for me in twenty years' time. And what of my nose? Will I morph into some bulbous, ruddy Pinocchio? Are all men destined to become the BFG?

When 'problems' befall a man with even one iota of insecurity about his appearance, the tendency is to find similar 'faults' in those around him. This probably comes from a desire to feel accepted, normal or at least not alone with their 'condition'. Take baldness. One of my very good friends has started to lose his hair. Unlike the crop circle I now sport, his hair is receding to a traditional widow's peak. Although he never speaks about his hair loss (and it is tacitly understood amongst everyone that we must never talk to him about it – he would lose it completely, and I'm not talking about hair!) it's clear he feels very self-conscious. The poor bloke is struggling because he's just noticed his first symptom of getting older (not getting old – he's only thirty-three – there is a difference). So he looks for reassurance by pointing out the hair loss of every similarly blighted man he sees. He's developed a forensic instinct for detecting anyone disguising hair loss – Bobby Charlton comb-overs, Gordon Ramsay's brush-forward-and-ruffle, Paddy McGuinness's shave it short and stand tall so nobody notices the bald patch – he spots them all. Classic behaviour of a man approaching manopause.

For many men, the manopause is a war that must be fought on two fronts – not only are you losing the hair on top of your head, you're also contending with all manner of unseemly growths sprouting below it. For me though it feels like my own personal autumn: everything is heading south, falling out or dropping off. And unlike the men battling sudden spurts of body hair in places that were never hairy before, I am losing hair all over . . . I kid you not, my right leg has started to go bald. My shin is now as smooth as a baby's bum. The eleven hairs I've had on my chest since adolescence remain, but I expect their time too is almost up. If you were to see me naked you'd be forgiven for thinking I was a balding albino chimp tanned only on the face and hands, where TV make-up has been painted on. And no matter how long I spend on that bloody Slendertone, the search for 'Abs' has left me with just a mini fold of flab on an ever-loosening tum.

I notice that my energy levels are nowhere near what they used to be. The enthusiasm for life remains, as does the ambition, drive and determination. And now that I've been around for a while, I can bring some experience to bear on any situation. But I've got to admit I can't keep up with all the young whippersnappers that populate the TV corridors I pace. They look young and fit and ready to take on the world, while I feel like I've done ten rounds and am starting to crumble.

And, coming late to TV, I know my slide into old age will

happen in the unforgiving glare of the media spotlight. This throws up some interesting dilemmas for me. Obviously being on television, I have to think about how I look. I'm sure there's many men out there who will greet the slowing of their metabolism with a beer, a pie and a shrug of their increasingly hairy shoulders. I on the other hand get told by TV producers I must shape up to stop it looking like I'm decaying before the viewers' eyes.

I have had fistfuls of teeth fall out in the past couple of years – one even during a recording of my show. They still made me finish it and even had me say 'teenage pregnancy statistic' in one of the links, which was more or less impossible. Imagine Daffy Duck saying it and you will have some idea of the 'methhhh' I made of it. As soon as the tooth was replaced I was asked to consider having them whitened, and then having my gums treated for receding. Falling apart and growing fangs – all as a result of growing old. I am still waiting for the day when they order my face to be filled with a Simon Cowell smile – it won't be long now . . .

I have resisted all promptings to go for Botox. I can just about handle the hair lacquer and being dipped in creosote five times a week to maintain my on-screen tan (continuity, darlings, not vanity – honest) but I draw the line at Botox. It works for some but I'll stick with the laughter lines, crow's feet and four inches of foundation. Having a tight, taut head just isn't important to me. In fact those laughter lines have been earned and they're a permanent reminder of the good times; I don't want to airbrush them out of existence, in a desperate attempt to get back to an age I know I will never be again. And I can just about live with the deepening bags underneath my eyes. For now.

The last cycle of ageing I have to go through is old age itself. For this final stage of my life I look to my parents once more for what the future might hold. They are increasingly baffled by young people and new technologies (more on this later) and though they may not choose to acknowledge it yet, things are slowing down for them considerably.

My mum has a set of reading glasses she keeps upstairs in her bedroom. She only used to use them for longer periods of reading but now finds she needs them for everything from a newspaper to the post. Before getting to bed she needs them about four times each day but does she keep them close at hand? Of course not, she trails up and down the stairs four separate times to get them, replacing them in her bedroom each time. Crazy. Mum and Dad seem to follow each other around everywhere now, normally on a mission to find the latest set of Dad's lost pills.

Forgetfulness, frailty, bodily failures and a final acceptance that there's not long left will come to them as it will come to us all. Their passing will be devastating when it does happen but each of them will go, when the time comes, supremely loved by the other, missed by all around and rightly proud of a long life lived well, to the full and the highest of standards.

If TV decides that all I'm fit for after finally getting old and continually refusing Botox is being consigned to the Arlene Phillips Scrapheap then so be it. I will leave with my head held high, avoid any celebrity jungles and retreat to a life at home with the family and endless cups of cocoa. I am slowly learning what my parents have shown me all along: that there is nothing to fear from getting older. There is plenty to enjoy and lots more to look forward to. If I am trailing around after my wife in 30 years' time, fetching glasses that should always be kept in my pocket, hunting for tablets that should never have been lost but always, always so very in love, I'll know once again that I am the luckiest man in the world.

With my family all around me, a long life lived well and the ability to look back on it all and smile, I'll be content to know I survived puberty first, then the manopause and most of what life can throw.

2

Britain's Worst Mum?

During my time hosting *The Jeremy Kyle Show* I have come up against some truly shocking examples of poor parenting, and in too many cases a complete absence of any parenting at all. I reckon about half the guests I meet on the show have problems that come from the fact that their mother or father wasn't up to the task or couldn't even be bothered to try to raise them in the way all children deserve. Increasingly I find myself saying that some people just should never have been allowed to have children in the first place.

Every week my show is swamped with callers wanting to confront an absent parent, or worse, one who was there all along but only abused and neglected them. When I first started this job, horrific stories of abandonment would stay with me for weeks. Five years later, I find I've heard so many, all in their own way dreadful and shocking, that it is getting harder to remember details. They are steadily blurring into one. I hear stories that take my breath away because of their sheer cruelty so frequently, I've started to become a little hardened. I'm afraid I might become a bit immune to hearing the same thing over and over again – people creating life in this country without any thought for how they might go on to love, nurture and protect it. For a time I had genuine concerns that I was becoming desensitised. I thought I could no longer be shocked. But then I watched the *Ten O'Clock News* on Monday 16 November 2009.

The lead story that night was about Rebecca Stevenson, a 22-year-old who was dubbed 'Britain's Worst Mother' in the press. Why? Well, she, you may recall, is the woman who abandoned her four children to fend for themselves whilst she went out with friends on a twenty-four-hour drink and drugs binge. While her babies – and they were babies, aged four, three, one and three months – struggled to feed themselves in soiled nappies, this pitiful excuse for a woman saw fit to swill wine, cider and sambuca and snort cocaine. When they found the one-year-old, she was apparently 'hysterical' and 'soaking wet with urine' whilst the three-month-old was found lying in his own excrement with dried sick stuck to his hair! Rebecca was still in the local pub when they found the children, she'd boozed and drugged her way through the night and day without a second thought for the welfare of the poor little mites she'd left at home.

This story left me sincerely shocked, angrier, and more upset than any I've heard in years, and I wasn't alone. Anyone who knows my wife will agree that she can be as hard as nails! She's not prone to too many misplaced tears or any unnecessary fuss and nonsense but I walked in that night to find her weeping at the news on screen. What had really got to her was the fact that this tawdry excuse for a mother had left her four-year-old in charge. We have a four-year-old. And, at the time of writing, a five-month-old son for that matter. I could not imagine for one minute, leaving my Ava on her own in the house, far less in charge of my baby boy,

Henry. Neither could Carla, and it was trying to visualise that scenario that left her so upset. She was distraught. As she said to me, just how terrified must those children have been? Mother gone, who knows for how long, everyone crying, no food, no love, no attention and babies covered in sick and soiled nappies.

My blood is boiling again just thinking about it but what made my wife flee the room in floods was the image of the carnage that had been caused by the four-year-old trying to feed her one-year-old brother. She had leant a chair against the kitchen counter and clambered up onto surfaces dangerously cluttered with bottles, knives and broken glass to try and reach some formula. When police arrived on the scene, powdered milk was scattered everywhere. Chillingly, the footprints of the four-year-old had been trodden through the spilled powder as she struggled in vain to care for her family in a way that their mother had totally neglected to even try. This forlorn attempt to feed her baby brother had tragically failed, leaving him 'pale and grey, not alert and with a sunken head' when the authorities arrived on the scene.

This is beyond me. Surely we should be living in an era of extra vigilance. After the horrors of Baby P aren't we all meant to be doing more to protect the needs of children we know have been mistreated? In a case like this, in times like these, we have to look to the presiding judge to do what is right. This time though, the perpetrator of a dreadful crime against her own children was seen to get away with it, and with a court's blessing. Most galling to me were the words on the news that Rebecca Stevenson's 20-week suspended prison sentence was meant to be a 'deterrent'. I'm sorry but

I don't see what sort of a deterrent that is to Rebecca or anyone else. The defence lawyer said she'd abandoned her kids in 'a moment of madness' – twenty-four hours is a pretty long moment if you ask me.

Heartbreaking stories like this one confirm to me that kids having kids far too young do so without any forethought for the consequences. Rebecca Stevenson's four children have been fathered by three different men and she, by all accounts, was a young woman unhappy with her lot and struggling to cope. I get that she was in a tough place, made all the more difficult by neglecting to insist her sexual partners put something on the end of it. In one sense, she probably just wanted to have some fun, let her hair down and do the things other people her age enjoy, although of course there is world of difference between a good night out and a drink and drugs bender. I have no doubt that she probably regrets her actions. But can we guarantee that they will never happen again? How bad does an example of abuse or neglect have to be before we send someone to prison? How many second chances should society give a mother who so completely failed to take care of her babies? What if something goes wrong again? We can't say we weren't warned.

I guess we have to trust that those who made their assessments have come to the right conclusions for the welfare of those children but I for one can't quite believe that such appalling, willful neglect can seemingly go unpunished in this way. If your babysitter acted like that whilst in charge of your kids you'd want them thrown in a cell – a suspended sentence just wouldn't cut the mustard.

We hear all the time about good people desperate to have children who haven't been able to. Then there are the thousands of fine upstanding citizens who would make wonderful foster parents who are being denied that chance by acres of red tape and written off on piffling technicalities. Ask these people what they make of Rebecca Stevenson and the sentence she received for casting her children aside so she could get off her face and they, like me, might find it almost impossible to believe! You really couldn't make it up and that is just so, so sad.

3

'Doctor, doctor, give me the news,
I've got a bad case of being . . . RUDE!'

The first time we filmed an episode of *The Jeremy Kyle Show* outside the studio, I saw the very worst that 'Binge Drink Britain' has to offer. When I accompanied a Manchester ambulance crew on a Friday night shift, I was warned that it might get violent, at times I'd probably feel threatened and that most of the situations we'd be called to would be alcohol related. I knew I would be surprised or even scared but nothing prepared me for the shock of what was to follow. Or the disgust.

I expected to see drunken yobs and thugs. I expected to see grown men smashing glasses, trashing pubs and bashing each other. And depressingly, I did see all of that, but the most shocking thing I encountered that night was the behaviour of a supposedly respectable businesswoman in her mid-forties. She had obviously begun the day a well-dressed professional but she was horribly worse for wear by the time we arrived. We were called to her assistance after a drunken fall and charged with the task of getting her back on her feet and safely home. Fat chance!

This woman was abusive from the start. Expletives filled the air as she was helped off the floor and hauled onto the bed in the ambulance. My crew, the medical crew and even concerned bystanders were roundly hissed and spat at – just for trying to help. The tide of abuse was only stemmed when she started being sick. For sixty minutes a specialist team who might otherwise have been looking after a pensioner having a heart attack or a panicked young mum giving birth were instead obliged to nurse a pitiful, spiteful drunk who resisted every kind word or caring gesture offered to her. She was too drunk to figure out how to use her mobile and was so incoherent with booze that it was impossible to get her address so the ambulance crew had no choice but to deliver her to the local hospital. There she dried out and sobered up, in a bed that could probably have been used for someone far more worthy, for the next eight hours.

You might think that after such unrelenting and completely undeserved abuse, our ambulance crew would be allowed to get back to their proper work – saving lives. But no, they then had to spend a further hour clearing up the carnage the woman had left behind, mopping up the aftermath of what looked like an exorcism – a sea of vomit that was about forty per cent proof!

Apparently this sort of thing happens all the time but I think it is a national disgrace. If it were down to me, I'd make sure that ghastly woman was sent a bill to cover the costs of sterilising the ambulance and using a valuable hospital bed on a Friday night. The scary thing is that someone else-where might have died because an ambulance was stuck out on call with an idiot who, as far as I'm concerned, should have been left to sober up in a barrel of cold water.

In some countries, hospitals reserve the right to refuse treatment to any patient who is threatening or abusive to its staff. Apparently in some African countries, where they don't take the precious resources of medical staff for granted, if a nurse or doctor is abused by a patient then they can be ejected from the hospital, put to the back of the queue or sent somewhere else. I think we need a similar system here.

I know respect is something I bang on about all the time but if people can't find it within themselves to be polite and grateful for the free treatment being given to them to save their life, what hope is there? Most nurses I've spoken to don't even ask for gratitude. Despite poor pay and tough conditions, they will continue to care for anyone, anywhere, no matter how thankless the task. They don't seek special treatment or over-the-top praise. All they want is to be able to go about their day without being abused or threatened. Now, I know hospital can be a scary place where emotions run high, but is that really too much to ask?

Some doctors and nurses are screamed at by the patients they ask not to smoke on the wards or tell that, wait for it, they can't book them a taxi to toddle off home! This just beggars belief. Everyone reads every day about how stretched NHS resources are and yet there are still all manner of selfish sods out there going ballistic at the very people who have helped them back to full health, just because they have had to wait an hour or so for the free ride home that came on the back of the free treatment received and round-the-clock attention enjoyed! Well boo hoo. I'm sorry, but if I was running a hospital in which a fully recovered patient let rip at one of my staff for not immediately sorting them out a taxpayer-funded taxi, I would tell them to stick it! Plonk them in the waiting room, invite them to make their own travel arrangements and get back to the business of saving lives. In fact, when there are people being denied life-saving, cancer-beating drugs on the NHS because they're too expensive, it makes you wonder why we fund taxis home at all.

NHS staff and resources are rightly under scrutiny as part of our country's belt-tightening. We all need to make more efficient use of a limited pot of money. But I think people's attitudes need to change. We are extraordinarily lucky in the UK to have the NHS. In many parts of the world, if you can't afford the eye-watering bills for medical treatment, then you can't have it. It's a precious resource and we ought to treasure, not squander it.

My mother always said, 'Manners cost nothing, dear,' and she's right. That's why I think we should bill people like that woman who drank herself into oblivion, wasting time and resources and refuse treatment to people who abuse staff. Medically trained professionals should not be forced to act as babysitters, taxi bookers or lackeys to ungrateful, foul-mouthed, abusive louts. Anyone who threatens or intimidates a doctor or nurse trying to do their best to help them should be made to clean up their own mess and pay from their own pocket for depriving their community of valuable services no doubt needed elsewhere.

4

Getting the Job

Established format requires experienced host to present national television show, five days per week. Preferred candidate will be female.

If ITV had run an advert in the local papers for the person they wanted to fill the hole Trisha had left behind, that would have been the long and short of it. According to what I was told as I went for a series of auditions and screen tests, Trisha's replacement was to be as near as damn it to the on-screen original her viewers had come to love. *She* was to be cool, calm and confident but above all, she was to be a she! Over roughly seven years, audiences had grown used to a woman kicking off ITV's daytime schedule at 9.25 a.m. With all the upheaval surrounding Trisha's departure, it was apparently thought that the transitional phase between her show and its replacement would run smoother if a woman, albeit a different one, retained the role of presenter. In short, the viewers weren't ready for a change of show, host *and* the host's gender. Oh dear. Buoyed up as my agent was by having landed me a try-out for the coveted slot, the odds seemed stacked against me and I began to wonder if I was just there to make up the numbers.

Trisha leaving ITV for Channel 5 has obviously been the making of me. Her departure left a door open to a veritable dreamland that I was lucky enough to eventually walk through. Given all I know now it is funny to look back and remember how I had originally cursed her for shocking us all with the decision to switch channels. Back then though, her surprise defection looked to have ballsed up my shot at the big time. You see, before I was ever invited by ITV to audition for them, I was already quite a way down the track in talks to do the same for Channel 5. They had for some time wanted to launch a rival to Trisha's ITV show and had begun sounding out various potential hosts. I was one of them and things were progressing quite positively until Trisha dropped her bombshell. Once she had, Channel 5 had an easy decision to make, one that completely scuppered all my hopes.

What would you do? You're a new channel looking to launch a brand new talk show and all of a sudden the best known, most experienced face in the British business pops up and declares herself available. They must have taken all of about three seconds to plump for her, and the pilot I had edged ever nearer to making at Channel 5 went out the window quicker than you could say 'lie detector'! The upshot was a potential opening at ITV but as I've said already, the word on the street was that they were looking for a like-for-like replacement, and quite a well known one if possible. That ruled me completely out of the running. Or so I thought.

At that time in my life I had just begun to start panicking about my job prospects. My broadcasting career had so far been as a radio presenter. The merry-go-round of job swaps in radio is constant and in the last round of musical chairs, I had lost my seat at Virgin. My best mate was my boss at the time and he was the one who broke the news that I was to be the casualty of the station's latest shake up. That was tough enough but five months on, I was still out of work. Having worked at most stations and on most networks but clearly not now wanted by any of them, I figured my goose was cooked. Jobless and with a new baby just arrived, the one vaguely promising work prospect on the horizon had been the Channel 5 show. Trisha took that and it seemed as though I was now to be ruled out of the race to replace her on the basis of having testicles, and unknown ones at that! It felt a little like I had been kicked right in them.

Still, preliminary auditions were going ahead for ITV and I got a call out of the blue that ultimately changed my life. It came straight through to me direct. A producer and well-known TV bigwig called Johnny McCune had somehow got hold of my mobile number and wanted me to come in for a screen test. He was lovely and urged me to give it a go. I had nothing to lose, so I gratefully accepted but when I got to the studios I realised I was probably about the fiftieth person they'd seen. They'd probably gone through their short-lists and back-ups without much luck. I figured I was probably Mr McCune's wild card, a shot to nothing and last roll of the dice!

Anyway, I got there and had to host part of what was a real behind-closed-doors show, just like the one I present now only not to be broadcast. The guests I spoke to were real, the issues they discussed were genuine and I was to be thrown in at the deep end to see if I could cope. The filming of this screen test took place on the old Paul O'Grady set.

I remember standing in the wings, nervous, and looking at his organ (from The Organ Game on his show!) as I contemplated what was coming next. My hair was too big, my suit was too small but even so, this poorly dressed fool with the big bouffant had to get out on stage.

Before I went on, Johnny McCune came over to give me the heads-up on two issues. Unlike the others they'd tested, I wouldn't be getting an autocue. I had to learn my lines because 'Parky' had apparently nicked all the autocues for a show he was filming in the next studio along! Next up he told me that with the guests being real people, bubbling with real emotions etc., there was a good chance they might storm off stage at any moment. Apparently in an earlier screen test a guest had done just that, only to be wrestled to the ground by a woman wanting to host the show full time! Blimey. Others, Johnny said, had just frozen, remaining stock still as the show they were meant to be hosting literally walked out the door! Right then, don't freeze and don't rugby tackle guests – got it. I was ready.

There were three cameras and an audience of about ten, made up of suited people looking suitably important. I did my 'reading' intro bit with the lines I'd learned earlier and went straight into a story that featured an anorexic girl who weighed about four and a half stone. Next out was her boyfriend, a lovely guy who was also a chef. All I did was talk and listen. They were both so engaging and their heartbreak so tangible that I just went over to them and chatted. I forgot that this was TV and, moreover, an audition that might lead to a much needed pay cheque. I just got stuck in, empathised and offered what advice I could. It was then and there that I first told a story which will be very familiar to regular viewers of my show. I told them how my brother was once married to a ballerina who suffered horribly with anorexia and force-fed herself cotton wool to trick her stomach into thinking she was full. The guests listened to this and they talked – to me and each other. Progress was being made.

Nobody ran off stage, nobody stormed out. It felt like it was just the three of us, having a very emotional talk through things. She welled up, he welled up, I welled up – we all welled up. There were people in tears everywhere so I did what anyone would do in that situation. I saw a Kleenex box to the side of the stage so I went and got some tissues for this young lady to dry her eyes on. The credits rolled there and then and soon we were all making our separate ways home. I wasn't quite sure of what had just gone on but I hoped it had been for the best for all of us. I hoped it was a cathartic experience for them, but for me I suspected that being the unwitting catalyst for a load of impromptu tears probably spelled the end of the road. I figured the TV-types watching probably wanted something with more razzamatazz than three adults sobbing in the centre of a stage. Apparently they did not. They called me the next day with the news that I was to film my own pilot, and get a proper shot at being Trisha's full-time replacement!

I have found in TV that initial bursts of good news are usually followed by what can seem like interminable waits for the promises made to be carried through. That is not a criticism so much as an observation. In this case I had done well and was told I was wanted. Then things went quiet as all the people at ITV beavered around in the background to put everything in place for a pilot to be recorded. These things take time of course and in that limbo period – with no guarantees from anywhere else – I accepted a job offer from out of the blue to present *Jezza's Confessions*, a late-night phone-in show for Capital Radio. It wasn't until many weeks later that the pilot was sorted and I was told I would be picked up from my radio show and driven to film it in Norwich, with an early start. My shift at Capital finished at midnight in Leicester Square so sleep before the biggest day of my professional life was clearly going to be at a premium.

The omens were not good. The car sent to collect me went to Virgin Radio, not Capital. D'oh! Once in the car, I was interrogated by an irritable driver who demanded to know if I was 'the one coming up to try and take over from *our* Trisha!' The last thing ITV had said was that *nobody* was to know who I was or what I was doing in Norfolk but this guy already knew everything. I later learned that the cab company ferrying me was the same one Trisha and her production office in Norwich had used for the past six or seven years. Not only was he on to me, he seemed to hold me personally responsible for stealing away Norfolk's darling of daytime TV. Whatever, word had got out. I thought ITV would cut my tongue out for blabbing so as the driver's questions kept coming I pretended to be asleep in the back of the car whilst in fact worrying about how I would cope with filming in the morning after next to no sleep at all.

I must have spent all of about an hour in a Norwich hotel before being picked up and whisked down to ITV Anglia's studios. There were people pacing up and down everywhere. This was clearly ITV's big punt to find a new face for their old show and they had pushed the boat out. Production staff buzzed about busily whilst I stood in the eye of the storm, waiting for some direction. About forty different people barked different instructions at me as they all got ready to film what would to all intents and purposes be the first *Jeremy Kyle Show*. The organised chaos and the huge behind-the-scenes efforts that go into making just one episode of a show like mine are scary when seen for the first time. There are so many people all flying around looking stressed. I am used to it now but back then it was all alien to me. It made me anxious, so I escaped to the roof to collect my thoughts with a lighter and about thirty cigarettes.

I was chain smoking by myself, trying to take in the enormity of the TV machine clunking noisily into life below me. Everyone was nervous. This was my one chance certainly, but for the entire production team, this was their big shot too. Trisha had gone and if this bombed most of them would likely be out of work. The tension was palpable and as I twitched on the roof a small man in black trousers and T-shirt casually strolled up to me. He looked fairly nonplussed by all the drama and I figured he might be someone from the crew or canteen, just taking a quick fag break of his own. He started the conversation.

'How's your day going? Hey, aren't you Jeremy Kyle?'

'Yes I am, and I'm having a terrible time. Between you and me,' I confided, 'I haven't got the first clue what I'm doing here. It's all going to shit!'

'So, why *are* you here then?'

'Well, one day I want to be Michael Parkinson!'

With that I turned on my heel and left to face my destiny. It wasn't until later that a producer pointed out that the 'cleaner' I'd been swearing at and confessing incompetence to was in fact *everyone's* boss. I'd probably just signed my own death warrant with the then ITV Director of Programming, Simon Shaps. Nice one, Jez.

The day passed by in a complete blur after that. I can't for the life of me remember the show, the filming, the guests or any of the stories we covered that day. All that really stands out was the fact that it all took place under Trisha's watchful gaze! In the studios where we filmed, pictures of her hung everywhere. Literally every five yards along every wall there was another huge portrait of her beaming back at me. Even in studio she was there. Before handing me my microphone the floor manager fixed me in the eye, not releasing his grip on it until he had whispered, 'This is *Trisha's* microphone.' I was left in no doubt I was on her patch and I scarcely dared speak into the mic in case I contaminated it in some way.

By some miracle, at the end of a long day's filming the general consensus seemed to be that things had gone well. Typically, that initial high was followed by another period of intense uncertainty. For about five months, I heard nothing. My highest hopes were once more dashed by a wall of silence and for ages I just didn't know where I stood. The rumour mill had gone into overdrive and there was lots of talk that Vanessa Feltz had been lined up for a triumphant comeback in the slot she had been forced to vacate for Trisha. The press reports at the time seemed to bear that out, too. They stoked my insecurities when I read that Vanessa was being trumpeted by those in the know as the most likely winner in a two-horse race for the job. I thought it was probably game over but ITV's own press statements were still saying that it was between 'a well-known name and a complete unknown.' I've been told since that Vanessa was never in the running. Obviously I was the complete unknown so who, I wonder, was the other well-known name in the frame?

Eventually, after what seemed like forever, I was invited down to London for a silver-service dinner at which the gods at ITV could run the rule over me. This took place up in the clouds on the twenty-first floor of Television Centre at Southbank. I didn't know then what a big deal this dinner date was but put it this way, I've not been back up beyond the sixteenth floor since! I was very polite throughout and did not stray beyond two glasses of wine, one more of which might have prompted me to leap on the table and yell, 'Look, are you going to sign me or not?!' It had been that long and the suspense was killing me but with no news and dinner done I said my goodbyes and left. Feeling a little deflated, I was on my way out of ITV when I received a call that put a fresh perspective on all of my petty frustrations.

Irene, my mum's only sister and my only aunt, phoned me, distraught. Her husband had just been diagnosed with cancer. She gulped back tears as she explained that he was now staying in Guys Hospital. As I was in London too, I promised to stay in town over night and meet her by his bedside the next day. It was as I was dashing to do just that, legging it out of the Tube at London Bridge, that Grant, my wonderful agent, called demanding to see me. I tried to put him off and told him I had to be with my aunt but, unusually for him, he was insistent. 'I *need* to see you!' was all he said. He sounded a bit desperate. More problems?

I arranged to meet him an hour after my visiting time with Aunty Irene, in a pub called The Grapes just outside the hospital. But my time in the hospital was so overwhelming, I forgot all about it. There were hugs, tears and tightly clasped hands as we all sat across my uncle's bed, promising each other that things *would* be alright, that as a family we'd all be there for each other and that we *would* get through this. I was glad to be there and offer some support but I left feeling drained.

I headed back to the Tube and walked straight past The Grapes without it even registering that my agent was inside with some apparently big news. My phone bleeped with a text as I was about to descend the escalator to the Underground trains. 'Where are you?' my agent wanted to know. Damn! I bolted back to The Grapes and rushed in to see him looking very sombre. Oh no, not good.

He asked me what I wanted to drink. I pleaded with him to get me nothing more taxing on the senses than a Coke and told him where I'd just been. I warned him that I was not in the mood for bad news and told him that this was already turning out to be a very draining day. Having left him with that thought, to go to the toilet, it was a little shocking to find him nestled at a table with a gleaming silver bucket stuffed with ice and champagne when I returned! He could obviously see that I was not in the mood to be toyed with and before I gave him a mouthful for being so insensitive with his drinks order, he just blurted it out.

'You've got the job!'

What job? My head was still spinning.

'Jez, you've got the job. At ITV. They've signed you up for thirty episodes. Congratulations!'

And with that, it seemed the deal had been done. The moment had arrived. It really was happening after all this time, and on today of all days. I slumped back in my seat, reeling slightly from the day's emotions and tried to let this latest bit of news get properly processed by my disbelieving brain. I exhaled, looked up and was probably more than a little misty-eyed as the moment washed over me. (Note to self – must stop crying through Life's big moments!) It was only then that I noticed a framed photograph above my agent's head.

It was a picture of Her Majesty the Queen Mother and it commemorated a visit she had made to The Grapes, perhaps even to open it. I gazed at the photo for a while and then I saw him. Just coming into frame, and beside the Queen Mother as he had been for so many years working in her service, was my Old Man. He was in the picture that was looking down on us. The biggest moment of my career to date and my dad had somehow been there watching over the whole thing – probably making sure I was happy and OK, just as he always has.

5

Lies, Damned Lies and True TV

It seems that pretty much everyone has a wish list for their ideal dinner party or get-together in the pub. Most of my friends have at some point debated which six people – past or present, famous or not – they would like to host for an evening fuelled by good food, fine wine and unending banter. Most people's guests are lifelong heroes, figures admired or hated by history, one impossibly beautiful heartbreaker and Stephen Fry. Always Stephen Fry.

The part of the evening that everyone would most look forward to, I'd wager, is that bit towards the end of the dinner when guards drop and inhibitions are cast aside. Basically, when the wine has taken hold!

Nobody likes the awkward small talk at the start of an evening but everyone enjoys that tipping point when lips are loosened, the moment when people feel comfortable and start being their true selves. Say you'd invited a Prime Minister – I know lots of people who wouldn't much fancy braving *that* smile while exchanging stiff early evening pleas-antries with Gordon Brown but quite a few who'd relish giving him a grilling over dinner, once they were two bottles of red to the brave. There's many who'd love to gawp at

Angelina Jolie across their candlelit dining table but not a lot who'd actually be able to speak to her without some Dutch courage.

I've always had a habit of asking impertinent questions way ahead of schedule. It has got me into trouble a few times before. If I want to know something about someone I tend to just come out and ask. I don't wait for an appropriate amount of time to pass and I've never needed alcohol to kick-start a conversation. At my ideal dinner party I wouldn't waste time building confidence over a few drinks, I'd get straight in there, asking whoever whatever and finding out the *real* story behind rumours or scandals. And, annoying sod that I am, I'd keep chipping away until they told me.

Now, some people might consider it the height of rudeness to have a lie detector expert on hand to test the guests at your party, and I suppose on the whole, I can see that it might be a bit off-putting. However, for that *ideal* dinner party, and that one chance to ask questions and get to those admissions that Truth or Dare just can't reach, I think I'd do it. My guests would be escorted upstairs one at a time to sit a lie detector test in the spare room, and everyone could discuss their answers over dessert!

I am writing this chapter about six months away from a general election. Today I watched Chancellor Darling (before those 'forces of Hell' were unleashed I always used to imagine Gordon Brown summoning him gruffly before sending him on his way with a pat on the bum and a huskily whispered, 'Thank you, Darling' – I blame *Blackadder*) deliver a pre-Budget report that most observers were saying will shaft as many people as possible in order to dig us out of the hole created by the bankers and/or the current government, depending on who you believe. And it's that last bit, 'depending on who you believe', that is causing me the most trouble.

All day long my opinions have been smashed back and forth across a political tennis court because I don't know who to believe. I can't work out who is telling the truth. I started the day chiming with the view that the government has been in charge for twelve years and therefore must be responsible for our financial strife. 'No more boom and bust' we were promised and yet here we are in the middle of the biggest recession since the thirties, and a bust bigger than Jordan's. 15-Love, the Tories. Later, Brown and his Darling went on to list everything they say they have done to alleviate child poverty, to help unprecedented numbers of people into work and how none of this would have been possible under the Tories. New Deal, Minimum Wage, sounds credible – 15-All. Then the Tories come back and point out that one in five of our young people is unemployed and we have the highest jobless total in decades. Can't argue with that: 30-15, Tories. And so it goes on. Claim and counter claim, all based on 'facts' that show black is white or white is black depending on who you're cheering for. As far back as I can remember, I've been watching two people giving polar opposite assessments of the same political situation on TV and on each occasion I have been left thinking that one of them must have been lying. It was exactly the same today.

On my show I am regularly confronted with a similar dilemma. One person will come on and accuse the other of doing something despicable like cheating on them. The other will come out and refute the allegation totally and both will wheel out all manner of evidence that 'proves' their point.

Invariably I look to a lie detector to sort out fact from fiction and judging by the amount of confessions we get backstage after a guilty result has been revealed, they are remarkably good at getting to the truth of a situation. I wonder if they couldn't be employed on shows like *Question Time* to help idiots like me have a clearer understanding of just who we can trust from the political classes.

I wish we could set up True TV, a company that would settle these petty political squabbles once and for all, right before our very eyes. If TTV were overseeing *Question Time* they could have the *real* stats and therefore the truth behind every topic ready at hand. If a slick-rick politician tried to sell us any un-truth that couldn't be supported by proper, independently assessed data a buzzer would go off. They would be bathed in red spotlight and the panel in front of them would flash 'LIAR! LIAR! LIAR!' as a siren sounded. They would have been outed and us at home would know that MP was not to be trusted. In fact, even better, why not gunge them as well, just like a Bushtucker Trial? I'm (half) joking of course, but only because it's so hard to distinguish between different versions of what is really going on in the country.

It seems unbelievable to me that we have to guess our way to electing a new government. Each day on the news programmes we watch people paraded before us, knowing they're probably deliberately deceiving us and yet there's no way for the average man in the street to know which ones to trust. In the last few years we've had a Prime Minister start an allegedly illegal war on false, 'sexed-up' grounds, MPs claiming money for porn, duck houses and moat cleaning and yet still, at the time of writing, no real sign that Parliament is going to clean up its act.

I'm always amazed when I watch the theatre that is Prime Minister's Questions. One wobbly overweight MP will slag off his equally rotund counterpart and put a 'fact' to his 'right honorable friend'. The 'friend' will retort with much huffing that said fact is false and offer other 'facts' on the same subject to prove that his party is right and everybody else is wrong. The entire House of Commons is jeering, waving papers and snorting like hogs in the trough, faces strangled red by too-tight ties. It really is an unbelievable spectacle. Every time I've watched our MPs in this Wednesday afternoon free-for-all, I've wished I could press the red button on my remote and have some subtitles, or better still an all-knowing political oracle pop up to tell me the truth about who was selling me down the river with another pack of lies.

That may never happen and, sadly, I doubt *Question Time* will ever embrace gunge tanks . . . That said, I still have my show and I'd welcome any of our political élite on to face the lie detector. It would be a bit like watching *Newsnight*, only with lie results at the end. 'Right Honorable Friend' 1 walks on and accuses the other of X, Y and Z. 'Right Honorable Friend' 2 waddles out, indignant, and accuses his contemporary of this, that and the other. We send them off for a lie detector and get the results after the break. Did you fiddle your expenses? Did you take us to war illegally? Did you goose your secretary? Have you ever lied to Parliament? How many times have you knowingly lied to the country? We could answer them all – I'd certainly watch. Moreover, by the end of the show I'd actually know who I should and should not believe in future.

Somehow though, I can't quite see it happening, so I'll have to go back to the drawing board for my ideal dinner party and forever wonder how it might've turned out. And just for the record, I would invite Margaret Thatcher, Tony Blair, the Queen, Simon Cowell, Paul Burrell and my dad. If they came round, I'd knock them up some chicken nuggets, no problem. I'd even crack open a bottle of Blue Nun but they'd not be getting any dessert until they'd all gone upstairs to my spare room and faced their own moment of truth with a lie detector test . . .

Margaret Thatcher and the Queen famously never got on and Her Majesty was apparently incensed when Maggie announced, royally, that 'we have become a grandmother' when her son's wife gave birth. Paul Burrell was saved at the last minute by the Queen when it seemed he would go to jail for helping himself to some of Princess Diana's possessions. My dad worked in the Royal Household for over thirty years and he detests the man – though he has never felt able to tell me why. He'd have a whale of a time at this do and I might uncover the source of his ire, too.

Tony Blair I would love to chat to, after a wee Iraq-based interview upstairs of course. I'd like to get a sense of whether there was any substance behind all that spin of his and just how many lies he knowingly told, and to what end. What was his real motivation? Liberation? Pleasing George Bush? Fame?

Finally, Simon Cowell. I could just hang back with him, watching as the night unfolded, plotting how we might make millions from our little gathering. No Stephen Fry of course, but I guess he'd be busy anyway, attending the ideal dinner parties of almost everyone else in Britain.

6

Fuming in a Winter Wonderland!

Oh, the weather outside is frightful . . . and so begins another of those songs we all croon each Christmas, romantically hoping that the coming festive season might be made all the more perfect by a light dusting of snow. Most of us are guilty of 'dreaming of a white Christmas' at some point, safe in the knowledge that the nearest we're likely to come is another day of unrelenting Great British drizzle. The kids are worse. Mine do frenzied tribal dances for it, praying for the stuff in the hope that they might get to build snowmen in the garden instead of going to school. *Let it snow, let it snow, let it snow* indeed.

Personally, I'll never again be singing for snow at Christmas. *Bah humbug* me all you like, but this country just can't cope with those wintry pictures promised on our Christmas cards each year. One quick blast of Baltic blizzards in 2009 was all it took for Great Britain to be reduced to quivering gridlock. For Berkshire where I live, read Narnia. It is 21 December, the Snow Queen reigns and Jack Frost is not so much nipping at my nose as getting right on my tits!

What is it about this country? We are famous for our weather's capacity to serve up four seasons in one day. We

congratulate ourselves for having the best of all meteoro-
logical worlds and bask in changing seasons that are the envy
of many. We have so much wonderful weather to celebrate
and yet we seem uniquely incapable of coping with any of
it.

We can be right royally pissed on for nine months solid,
river banks breached, homes flooded, population bedraggled
and yet at the first sign of sunshine, what happens? Hosepipe
bans are suddenly the order of the day. If the sun puts his
hat on and gives us anything like a proper summer, the roads
start melting. Air conditioning fails on trains, people pass
out on Tubes and the people in charge say 'sorry mate, it's
not our fault, we weren't properly prepared.'

Come autumn and the rail network grinds to a halt because
of leaves on the line. It doesn't matter that leaves have been
falling from trees since time began, that we know they will
continue to fall this year and next, or that no other country
in the world finds the clearing of them from their tracks a
problem, for Great Britain it's always a catastrophe. 'Sorry
mate, it's not our fault, we weren't properly prepared.'

Fast forward to winter and if any snow falls then the
country will grind to a halt once more. In 1991 we had the
'wrong sort of snow' and in 2009 we had too much of it.
It's just unbelievable: the UK, a fully developed G8 nation
supposedly at the forefront of modern technology and we
were in absolute chaos because of a bit of snow! This time
we were even meant to be prepared for it, we were certainly
warned well in advance that snow was on the way.

I watched *BBC Breakfast* on the morning of Thursday
17 December 2009. Throughout their broadcast they carried
live reports from a gritting depot that was swinging into

action to help the nation combat the incoming cold. The government had declared there was plenty of salt to grit the roads, the local councils had their extreme weather emergency plans in place. Everyone seemed to be confidently proclaiming that this time we were indeed ready. The kids might miss school and get to go sledging in the park but for the rest of us, Britain was open for business as usual. My children would get to build their snowman but daddy would still be able to get to work. That was the plan; that was the promise . . . Four days later I was sat here typing, wondering when or if I might ever see my wife or children again.

On Monday 21 December 2009 Carla and our three children (aged 6, 4 and 8 months at the time) left home to do a bit of Christmas shopping. They only went to Camberley, about six miles away. They left just after lunch and by all accounts had a great time going to grottos and looking for last-minute stocking fillers. They left while it was still light, eager to beat the rush and get home in good time. My wife was happy and the children, all dosed up on sugar and Santa, typically manic. They left Camberley at about 3 p.m., what time do you think they made it home? Twenty past eleven at night!

I'm sorry but this is ridiculous. Carla said there had been some sort of car accident on the icy roads and she had been stuck in traffic for hours. Driving, when she was finally able, was treacherous. Carla was scared, the kids, tired, hungry and probably sensing their mother's fear, began to scream. My wife rang me to keep me informed and it sounded like bedlam in the car. I was out of my mind with worry as my family sat tantalisingly out of reach a few miles down the road, dining only on a tear-stained packet of biscuits that

47

were originally intended for Father Christmas's tum, after he'd made it down our chimney. Thankfully they did finally make it back. Traumatised no doubt, but safe and sound nonetheless.

Once we'd put the kids to bed, Carla finally let rip and she was quite right to do so. Where were the gritting lorries we'd been told to expect? This weather was no harsher than the routine winter conditions we see most years in February. And it certainly wasn't a surprise – it had been the only thing on the news for four days running! Why was it causing such a problem? Why, again, were we so bloody unprepared?! With council taxes going through the roof and every other tax imaginable set to rocket too, hadn't we a right to expect more? So much for the council's promises of preparedness, they all sounded like Gordon Brown's boast to have ended boom and bust, just before he ushered in the longest recession since records began. Thanks a lot!

We weren't the only ones to suffer. A friend of mine spent 18 hours of his pre-Christmas trip to Bruges stuck in traffic snarled up outside the British end of the Channel Tunnel. Typically, he reported, the weather was worse on the other side but for some reason it was only here in Blighty that the weather caused complete and utter chaos. They simply got on with things on the Continent but over here there was gridlock. And he was one of the 'lucky' ones. At the same time he was crawling home along our ice-rink roads, about 55,000 people were stranded on platforms in London, Paris and Ashford. Eurostar services had been cancelled for three days after six passenger trains had broken down in the Tunnel in one single night. The problem? Well, in layman's terms, condensation caused by going from the cold outside the

Tunnel to the warm inside had messed with the trains' electrics and they had broken down as a result.

It took some people about four days to get home after that debacle – all because of a bit of cold weather. I can only imagine how hard and horrifying that ordeal must have been for those stuck in the Tunnel and then stranded on the other side. My wife was strung out and my kids petrified after 'just' eight hours stuck a few miles from home. I shudder to think what it must have been like on those broken down Eurostar trains.

Look, don't get me wrong. I understand that Mother Nature will always hold the whip hand over the best laid plans of mice and men. At some point extremes of weather will beat whatever we do to try and combat them. However, what I can't understand in this day and age is that we in this country can't withstand a few minor fluctuations on the temperature gauge without the whole country going into paralysis. If six inches of snow suddenly fell in downtown Delhi I'd expect there to be a bit of a panic about what to do, but it's not like Britain has never seen a blizzard. And let's be honest, the snow we did see was nothing compared to the Arctics and Alaskas of this world. Countries right around the globe experience worse extremes of temperature than we ever will and they seem to cope fine, so why is it always us that is so caught out whenever the weather changes? And if we're so incompetent why can't we just ask someone who can actually deal with it to give us a helping hand? Ask our man in Moscow how their airport stays open when the temperature hits minus 30 or anyone in Spain about the mystery of un-melting motorways when the mercury tickles its way above 20 degrees. People elsewhere clearly know how it's done so let's get some of that expertise on board over here.

That friend of mine said that when he left Bruges it was far colder than the UK, the snow much deeper and yet the trains were running to time. Every disgruntled Frenchman interviewed at a Eurostar terminus seemed shocked that something as everyday and mundane as a bit of cold could cause such widespread disruption. Tellingly, most Brits just shrugged their shoulders with all the resignation of natives used to the failure of their authorities.

I have no doubt normal service will soon have been resumed for everyone I've watched on the news. For those on the Continent that will mean a return to efficiency and punctuality of services, the likes of which we can only dream about. For us it will likely mean another brief reprieve before the change in season brings about more travel misery, for which we will no doubt be obliged to pay ever more steeply. And soon enough everyone will be digging out the tinsel and singing hopefully about the prospects of 'walking in a winter wonderland'. Not me though. I could handle being snowed in when everyone returns to work in January but the next time someone talks nostalgically about their dreams for a white Christmas I'll remind them of the millions of people who had their plans to be with loved ones dashed because we couldn't cope with a bit of adverse weather. Of all the songs to be sung for those who couldn't get back to where they needed to be in 2009, perhaps this Yuletide hymn was most appropriate:

'In the bleak midwinter
frosty wind made moan . . .'

Bleak it may be if the snow returns next Christmas as it did the last, and moan I certainly shall if I have to mount an Arctic expedition to retrieve my family from another un-gritted icy road!

7

Rage Against the Machine

Don't you just love the Great British Public? Just when I thought we might be sleepwalking towards society's Armageddon, just when I thought that everyone had stopped caring about the outrages splashed across the papers each day, just when I thought we'd surrendered all sense of independence to the State, I got a perfect reminder of how uniquely Great the British public really is.

There are inquiries into illegal wars, crooked politicians on the make, bandit bankers on the take. The planet's melting, the country's going bust, everyone's losing their jobs and still we accept billionaire bonuses going to those who ruined the economy on the one hand and millions being creamed off the State by certain undesirables on the other. I know everyone huffs and puffs about the state of this country but all too rarely does anyone seem bothered enough to stand up for change.

Therefore, isn't it heartening to know that there are still a few people out there who refuse to be pushed around? No matter how blinded or apathetic we may have become, the decent folk of this country can still rise up and stick it to the Man. There's nothing we like more than an underdog and when big business or those in power get the odd bloody nose, no one cheers louder than me.

Take show business for example. The warning's pretty clear: get too big or too popular and you'll find dissenters everywhere. The people who loved you at the beginning and helped build the brand will soon start turning against you if your star rises too high. I've experienced the backlash myself. Believe it or not, I was once welcomed as a breath of fresh air on TV by many of those who now queue up to bash me on a daily basis.

And now there are signs the tide might be turning for Simon Cowell, who has for so long been the adored ruler of our TV kingdom. For the last five years or so, Mr Cowell has been the dominant media force on both sides of the Atlantic. He has been delivering record audiences with *American Idol, Britain's Got Talent* and *The X-Factor* and, nasty or not, we've all taken him to our hearts. I met him once and have to say I was very impressed. He was charming, gracious and very generous with both his time and some sound advice. Best of all was the aura he had around him; he was in total control of the room. I have nothing but admiration for the man and all he has achieved but even so, and despite my personal experience of his niceness, there was still something quite reassuring about the campaign to oust one of his protégés from the Christmas Number 1 slot in 2009. For four years running, the eventual *X-Factor* winner had been a shoo-in for the top slot in the festive charts but last year Britain said, 'No more!' Nineteen million people tuned in to watch Joe McElderry's *X-Factor* victory, but waiting in the wings to rain on his parade was a resistance mobilised by two everyday Brits sat at home on their computers. Fed up with Simon Cowell's apparent strangle-hold and disillusioned with the annual carve-up that had seen his talent show winners blitz their way to Number 1 each year, Jon and Tracy Morter launched a campaign to redress the balance. Unbelievably, they did it.

The Morters toppled Geordie Joe after encouraging over half a million of their Facebook followers to buy Rage Against the Machine's very festively titled 'Killing In The Name Of'. The final refrain of that ditty was I think aimed at the TV and tabloids backing Joe. *'F**k you, I won't do what you tell me!'* screamed RATM, 'F**k you, I won't buy what you sell me!' was the message sent to Simon and Co. Fair enough. Although the irony was not lost on me – thousands of people raging against those who follow the herd and buy a certain song make their point by following *another* herd and buying *another* song – I did rather admire the Little Man's triumph in upsetting Big Business's established order of things. Don't unquestioningly gulp down everything spoon-fed to you. Make a stand for what *you* think is right! Well done, Great Britain.

I don't much care about all the hype that surrounded this battle and didn't really understand why some people got so worked up about it. What I did like though was the pluck the Morters showed in fighting against the odds (150-1 at one point!) for what they believed in. It makes me puff up my chest a bit prouder to think that this little island of ours won't always blindly go along with expectations.

I also can't help but smile when I remember the thou-sands who teased Simon further by continuing to vote for singing twins, Jedward. It was the same a little while back, on *Strictly Come Dancing,* with the campaign to preserve

John Sergeant, much to the annoyance of Angry Arlene Phillips, the woman who'd labelled him 'a dancing pig in Cuban heels!' This country has always celebrated the eccentric and the odd novelty act of naffness. And it will back them with votes or hard sales. How else do you explain Mr Blobby once having a Christmas Number 1, or Bob The Builder or even Cliff Richard having three? One of the things I love most about this country is its ability to laugh at itself. Combine that with our occasional capacity to snap back when we've all had enough of corporate tyranny and you'll see why Simon Cowell came a Christmas cropper or perhaps even how the legend that is Boris Johnson ever ended up as Mayor of London!

Mind you, just as our unique wit and appreciation of irony underpins a pride in our national identity at one end of the scale, so there is a pettiness and small-mindedness that persists in undermining it at the other. Everyone has had an encounter with a schoolteacher, traffic warden or, worse, some Health & Safety yellow coat who has taken it upon himself to organise the universe with nothing but a clipboard, a large bunch of keys and a whining voice. You know, the sort of person that used to bark at you to keep off the grass at school whilst marching self-importantly across it himself. A sort of frustrated trainspotter meets Mr Bean. Well, I recently read a bizarre story that perfectly depicted the battle that will always rage between 'them' and 'us'.

A twelve-year-old pupil was excluded from his school by the headmaster for selling contraband items such as crisps and chocolate to classmates. Previously and rightly, this young boy's school had adopted a 'healthy food policy' which barred the sale or consumption of the sorts of salty, sugary snacks that all kids love a little more than they should. Apparently this boy was pocketing up to £15 a day from his peers, who were prepared to pay over the odds for the forbidden snacks, charging them a 10-15p supplement each time.

Now, I know the school was right to enforce a regime that would see their pupils fitter and better nourished as the country faces an obesity crisis. I also know that the boy should not have broken the rules – no excuses, no problem, it was a fair cop. That said, I have to confess I rather liked his spirit of endeavour and enterprise. Something inside me was cheering for him, just as it had cheered for Jon and Tracy Morter.

If I had been that headmaster I would have had to penalise him too. I would have had to be that uncool, seemingly uncaring authority figure that stuck to the rules, just as I am when disciplining my own children if they have gone a bit too far. Disciplining kids is the kindest thing to do in the long run, otherwise they have no boundaries. That said, I'm not sure I would exclude the boy as they did. Surely it is better to have a punishment that truly fits the crime? Shouldn't schools come up with sanctions that stimulate as much as they stifle? Otherwise kids like this enterprising young lad will get labelled a troublemaker when surely, in these stricken times, his entrepreneurial spirit should be fostered and nurtured.

They should have given him a detention in which he was forced to apply his obvious business know-how for the benefit of his classmates or local community. Simply chucking him out of the school smacks of taking the easy (or lazy?) option. Yes, give him extra lessons on diet and fitness but why not also have him hone his sales skills by selling raffle tickets for the school, or helping with a campaign for a local charity – don't just kick him out and send him home!

The poor boy will have learnt a tough lesson – but I hope he can take the positives from his experience, too. In business as in life he will come up against a lot of people who won't like what he is selling or perhaps even the way he is selling it. He'll soon learn that he has to be just that bit more ingenious to make his fortune within the rules. And I have no doubt he can. Like the Morters, I see him as another of this country's underdogs with outstanding potential. They were David standing up to Goliath, as he may yet be a business Goliath in the making – a young man ready to come back from his own bloody nose and go laughing all the way to the bank . . . just like a certain Mr Cowell!

8

The Jeremy Kyle House of Horrors

Does anyone remember playing *Whack-a-Rat,* the game that used to stand out front at amusement arcades? It basically involved a player having to bludgeon any rodent that dared to poke its head up through one of a series of holes. He or she who was most merciless with their mallet would usually emerge the winner, much to the amusement of all around who'd gather to watch the player's contortions as they dealt out death to smiley-faced vermin.

I recently read that the game had been updated to reflect the mood of our times. *Whack-a-Rat* has become *Bash-a-Banker* in some arcades but while the figures have undergone a makeover the game has remained the same: dementedly chase each pop-up creature like some mad Matron from a *Carry On* film and 'whack' it with your mallet before it retreats, only to emerge and mock you once more. Towards the end of the playing time the game gets feverish with 'rats' popping up everywhere at breakneck speed like some sort of crazed frog chorus on fast forward. The player becomes overwhelmed with too many rats to whack, too little time left to whack them and basically needing to be some sort of octopus just to keep up.

I haven't played *Whack-a-Rat* in years but recently I experienced exactly those same emotions. I wasn't in an arcade this time, there were certainly no amusements around, and the tide I was fighting desperately to keep at bay was a steadily rising one of things best left for the toilet . . .

Anyone with children will know that illnesses regularly get handed back and forth between parents and kids. It can feel a bit like some sort of sick relay in our house, one in which every ailment gets passed round and round, for months on end. It gets to the point where it feels like nobody ever really recovers; they just get a temporary reprieve and then wait their turn for the illness to work its way around to them again. With this in mind, and the knowledge that I live with my wife and three children aged six and under, it should be easy to see why sniffles are pretty commonplace in the Kyle household. It's irritating but no big deal really, the odd cough or runny nose shouldn't faze a hardened father of four – it's nothing compared to what can lurk in their nappies! However, when proper illness strikes it can turn a home like ours into a real-life house of horrors. And it did – the last time we got back from a short holiday to Dubai.

It's not everyone's cup of tea but I love Dubai. At the end of a long run of filming there are few places better for me to escape to. We have friends who live out there, nobody recognises us and the whole place caters to exactly what our family wants and needs from a holiday. Carla is more than happy to go bargain hunting in the shops all day, I love to lose myself on the gorgeous golf courses and the kids will happily splash about in the pool with whichever of us is back at base. Perfect.

All was as we had hoped on our last trip. Good food, great

time: perfectly relaxing for us parents and fantastic fun for all the kids, too. It wasn't until we stepped off the plane at Heathrow that we first had some sense that the good times just enjoyed were about to come to an abrupt end.

My body seems to intuitively know when it can and cannot get sick. It is almost as if my immune system works in sync with my work schedule. Coughs, colds, sniffles and sneezes can all be endured and never prevent me from going to work but the more grizzly stuff, the sort that keeps you bedridden or welded to the toilet, that stuff seems to know that it can only strike when work is done and the family is getting together.

Our mini-break to Dubai was over and we all headed home. Little did I know that my immune system was still on holiday, probably still out on the golf course. Within minutes of opening the front door it started. Tummy rumbles followed by whole torrents of nastiness gushing forth. I tried to quarantine myself and spent two days alone, either in bed sweating or contemplating the tiling patterns of my bathroom floor as I hunched over the bowl. I shut myself away to spare the family any similar suffering and I guess we all thought the problem had been isolated. I emerged forty-eight hours later, half the man I used to be, but assuming that everyone else in the house would be in the clear. How wrong could I be?

Next to drop and be barricaded in the master bedroom, which now doubled as the medical wing, was Carla. Bent double, sweating profusely and heaving from the boots up, it sounded like she was wrestling with a whole herd of farmyard animals in there. Again we thought we had contained the problem and again we were wrong. At some stage it had been passed from me to Carla and from Carla to our baby boy, Henry. Spewing and spraying like one of those fire hoses with a mind of its own, he contaminated his sisters, too.

Before I knew it, I was playing Florence Nightingale to one adult and three very young children. Having already lost half a stone when I suffered the bug, I set about losing another as I ran around the house mopping up mess. Scooping up bed clothes in one hand and ill children in the other, I scurried from one room to the other, checking on each patient and then the next. I had just enough time to mop brows or feed water to one before being shouted at to dash to another. I could almost hear the Benny Hill theme in my head as I tried to keep up. I've played pass-the-parcel but this was like pass-the-plague, and each time the music stopped, Daddy went in to play Mrs Mop!

Have you ever seen *Little Britain* where that bigoted granny vomits violently whenever homosexuals or ethnic minorities are mentioned? Well this was like that, if not worse. It was endless. I changed Ava's sheets four times in one night. I sat outside Henry's room at 2 a.m. with a bucket by my side, not knowing who to visit next or which member of my family was most in need.

Alice, my six-year-old, bless her, she needed Daddy to let her know it would be all right. Carla was pretty much fine doing shuttle runs to and from the toilet and Ava was typical Ava. Nonchalant to the last, she didn't seem much troubled by how sick she was. She flicked me a few looks of contempt as I tried to clean around her and went back to her business like this was just another day in the office for her. She's four years old! And Henry, whilst undoubtedly ill, seemed mostly unperturbed by this new adventure into violent illness.

You'll never meet a milder mannered, better tempered child than my boy. He would be sick, wail a bit and then go back to grinning and bouncing around in preparation for the next surge.

This living hell went on for about thirty-six hours in total. Sleep was at a premium and all around was chaos and confusion. It really was like the dying moments of a game of *Whack-a-Rat* as I worked myself into a frenzy, rushing around trying to clean everyone up. I seriously thought it would never end, but, finally, we did begin to shake off the worst of it and return to something approaching full health.

Order(ish) was soon restored and we reacclimatised to the madness that passes for normality at ours. The sheets were cleaned, the toilets scrubbed and I became a slightly obsessed Mr Muscle, spraying with disinfectant any nook or corner I thought might be the source of re-infection. And, as ever, no sooner had our time off begun than it had finished and I had to return to work feeling more than ever like all I needed was a holiday . . .

Still, every cloud – even those as noxious as the ones we were all emitting for most of the week – has a silver lining and it was my wife who spotted it first. 'Could be worse, Jez,' she said as she admired her newly enslendered curves in the hallway mirror. 'It would have taken me six weeks to lose that much weight at the gym and I've knocked off every cake I ate in Dubai in under two days!' Brilliant.

9

R.I.P. Off!

Nothing symbolised the widening gulf between this country's politicians and citizens more than the recent Commons' expenses scandal. To catch them with their greedy little snouts hogging through the trough was bad enough, but the failure of so many of them to see that they'd done anything wrong really was astonishing.

I'm sure everyone's had more than their the fill of hearing exactly how our elected representatives hoovered up any freebie they could get their grubby mitts on. I'll not labour the point here, but to me the only good thing to come out of the whole sorry saga was the shift in our attitude towards the political élite. Calling MPs to account has left many scurrying for their accountants. New blood seems to be on the verge of replacing blue blood in the chambers and an new era of transparency hopefully awaits. Out with the old, in with the new and let's start again with a wave of new politicians trying to make a difference on the back of a new mandate from what I hope will be a newly invigorated elec-torate. I hope by the time you read this that we have risen up and cleared out of politics those who were only in it for Queen and Country House. For the sake of faith in democracy I hope the general election was the catalyst for real change – in those we elect to represent us AND the way in which we demand they do so.

It's no wonder that people are angry and increasingly cynical in the wake of castle turrets fixed, duck houses bought and private moats cleaned, all at huge cost to a taxpayer purse we were told was empty. MPs are meant to be *our* public servants and yet they lorded it over us like kings, with a sickening sense of entitlement. As the rest of the country had their belts pulled tighter than a vest on John Prescott, the politicians who presided over an economic collapse that lead to the deepest, longest recession since the war kept dipping their fingers in our till. As everyone else faced job losses, pay cuts and house repossessions, our taxes were cynically syphoned into the fat-cat pockets of Members on the make. Where they should have been focused on sparing the people who put them into power from the worst of the hardship, MPs bumped up their pay with lavish expenses and looked after themselves. The economy fell in on itself but too many of our elected representatives found that they could help themselves to more than enough of our money to keep them laughing all the way to the newly nationalised banks.

Very few politicians seemed capable of grasping the scale of the anger, far less the real feelings of those being forced to struggle through tough times that were not of their making. Joe Public kept feeling the pain whilst the people with Seats kept conspiring to gain. Everywhere we looked, people of privilege were being propped up with undeserved loot that had been picked from our pockets. Millionaire bankers were bailed out with billions of our cash but still those obscene bonuses came back. For food – yes, food – MPs piled their plates high with £400 a month of tax-funded handouts, treating eating as a perk of Parliament that the rest of us somehow never have to do! A Home Secretary's husband even managed to buy porn flicks courtesy of the taxpayers' endless tab. (One of the films is alleged to have been *Raw Meat 3*, which goes under the tag line, 'It's the end of the world – and we blow it.' Oh, the irony.) I was as shocked as anyone by the craven self-service those expense claims revealed. And something important in my thinking shifted.

If we're honest, most of us would say that we've never trusted politicians or believed very much of what they say. However, deep down, I'd always thought that most of them went to Westminster with the best of intentions and at least the goal of doing well for the rest of us, not *only* themselves. Over the years I've been forced to forgive many a sleazy minister caught with his trousers down. I've got over count-less government mistakes that have cost this country consid-erably. I've also excused unbelievable examples of incompetence by balancing an individual's political failings against a presumed personal integrity that I thought would see everyone in office doing the very best they could to score successes for the good of us all.

For years I've been assuring myself that even the most disingenuous, deceitful or dishonest of politicians had some part of their heart in the right place. Ditto with idiot politicians, even the most stupid of whom I have tried to convince myself probably meant well but just got in over their heads. Now though, I am not so sure. Now the self-ishness at the core of so many we look to for leadership has been exposed, I have begun to wonder whether I was just a bit naive.

Obviously I have always known that dark arts are employed by ambitious politicians to haul themselves to the top and that they basically have to scrap, scrabble and scurrilously engineer their way up, but I also thought that the point of doing so was to make changes that would improve the lives of the many.

Mind you, the clues were always there. The sight of Tony and Cherie Blair squandering the political capital they gained over a decade in power to brazenly chase the corporate dollar from any American company willing to flash its knickers at them, really was quite vulgar to behold. That should have opened my eyes to the real motivations of some in Parliament. I should have known then that for some politicians it wasn't about the work they did or the good they could do.

I've always wanted to believe that all people, no matter where they are employed, would have the quality of their work noticed and rewarded. Good people should be recognised and compensated for the brilliance they bring to the table without the need to smugly trumpet their own achievements. Good work should partly be its own reward, especially where the service of the nation is concerned. How galling then to have those in power pillage and plunder the public purse while the country lurched from one crisis to the next.

I sometimes wonder what the Queen must have made of all this. We are bossed by Her Majesty's Government after all. Seeing the Blairs tart themselves for tips like low rent lap dancers and seeing her Parliament laid low by avarice must have left her feeling sick, like she'd been burgled by the butler! I hope she shares our anger, I hope she feels the hurt we all do at being so blatantly fleeced. More importantly, I hope she can wield some influence to get government in this country back on track because I think the tide is turning against all politicians, no matter which party. And this feeling won't subside until people see the back of the MPs who took them for a ride and some real change to the apparatus of government that currently seems to be set deliberately against them.

After everything that has happened, I think we really have come to a crossroads in the way people perceive politics. Apathy is rife and support for the political process is ebbing away. Fewer and fewer voters believe that the politicians we've voted in care anything about our concerns. There is a creeping suspicion that the culture of greed consuming those at the top has now filtered down to the administrations they've left to control us all underneath. The people are starting to turn, wondering if the authorities aren't just out for what they can get at our expense. Does the system they preside over now run in exactly their image, hammering the masses in order to raise revenue, filtering more money from our pockets to theirs?

I watched a debate on this recently and have to agree with Quentin Letts that it does seem that officialdom in this country has turned against the people it is meant to serve. No sane person would deny that tax needs to be collected to pay for the public services we all want to enjoy. It's just that the amount of 'tax' being constantly drained from every area of our lives is now causing huge concern. Petty, punitive fines are handed out willy-nilly and I suspect the reason has nothing to do with local councils wanting to provide better services. I think we are being deliberately targeted, hit harder and more frequently, solely to raise revenue to balance the books at City Hall.

Everyday, hardworking, tax paying, law abiding citizens are getting clobbered with all manner of ludicrous levies which are both expensive and insulting. Hefty fines, rabidly chased, are being handed out for any minor sin, from parking indiscretions to mistakenly using the wrong bin. We are coming to expect that the people we elected to serve us are now there to shaft us, pilfering whatever they can from the public's back pocket the first chance they get.

Up until very recently I had suspicions that this was the way our public servants were sliding but I still wasn't certain. Then the expenses scandal hit and suddenly my doubts were disappearing. Soon enough I had my proof. I'm going to retell the experiences of a couple of friends to show how increasing numbers of people in this country think that the system built to govern them now only exists to abuse them.

One friend is a man who lost his dad to the ravages of alcoholism. His father, despite his problems, had worked hard as a painter for the local council for the best part of thirty years. He rented a council property and always paid his bills on time. His son, my friend, was understandably upset about his dad's death but what happened at the hands of the local authorities in the immediate aftermath just left him floored.

My friend was quickly forced into clearing up all manner of messes his estranged father had left behind. The funeral he had to borrow to pay for was expensive, and the family who turned up to it were, in many cases, completely unknown to him. It's safe to say it was a pretty topsy-turvy time and one that stirred up a lot of uncomfortable feelings for him.

Now, I don't think it unreasonable to expect that the local authorities act with a little compassion and understanding at such a time. My friend didn't ask for any special treatment from anyone following his father's death but at the same time he did not expect to be so coldly told to conclude affairs that had nothing to do with him. The real pearler he told me was receiving a bill from the council that he was ordered to pay on his father's behalf. The charge? One month's rent in full for the property his father had vacated on account of being deceased. The reason? His father had failed to give the council a month's notice of his intention to leave the flat! Unbelievable.

Are we now expected to know the exact day we'll drop down dead? Can councils really charge a corpse a full month's rent? I might, just might, understand if there were millions left in the deceased's estate but my friend's father had nothing. He drank himself to death and died penniless. That was of no consequence to the local authorities though, they had a contract, they wanted their money and my friend had to pay it. Of course he could have walked away and left everything for the council to clear up but he wanted to do the right thing for his dad, one last time. In doing so he ran up debts he didn't need on a credit card he didn't want and was incredulous to see that the agencies he thought might be on hand to help were only there to get their share.

Another friend also had a painful bereavement made worse by over-zealous officialdom gone mad in this country. She tragically lost her brother in a traffic accident that devastated her whole family. I saw the trauma of this loss tear her apart and she said it took months for her relatives to even begin to come to terms with the huge hole left in their lives, far less start the process of moving on and trying to fill it. However, this lady is nothing if not amazing and together with her nearest and dearest they slowly began to find a reason to live for themselves and each other again. Never forgetting the love inspired by the man they'd lost nor discounting the hold he'll always have over them, they grieved, got better and started to make sense of the world once more. How sickening that all their progress should be shattered by another unfeeling intervention from a local council. A letter that shouldn't have been sent contained a bill that should never have been charged and it blew this family apart once more.

My mate said that the arrival of this letter set her mum back months. It cruelly tore the scabs off wounds that had only just begun to heal and left her devastated too. The letter contained an invoice from the agency called out to attend her brother's accident. Their job had been to secure the scene and clear up the debris afterwards. Given their knowledge of what happened, what they resorted to next was nothing short of deplorable. They sent a bill charging my grieving friend's brother – the deceased! – for the costs incurred in clearing up the accident that had killed him. Realising that they couldn't squeeze cash out of the dead, they forwarded the bill on to the home of his still distraught relatives without a second thought for the potential ramifications. Again, just unbelievable.

A true democracy is meant to be one 'of the people, by

the people and for the people'. But if things carry on like this we will be left with a system tainted, or more probably ruined. One that doesn't cater for our needs, our desires or any of our values. One that forces people to the lunatic fringes or maybe even away from politics altogether. None of us want that but equally, a democracy run 'by the politicians, for the politicians, against and at the expense of the people' is not one I want any part of either.

10

The Day I Nearly Died

Even the most 'me-me-me' of people who make their living in the public eye have days when they wish the guys thrusting the cameras in their face would just shove off. Yep, even for those who crave the attention most jealously, there comes a time when the lens they love becomes an object of loathing, at least temporarily. Many a model has recoiled in horror at what has been splashed across the tabloids. Airbrushed perfection on the front of a lads' mag can soon give way to the lumps and bumps more common to the rest of us, once a 'pap' snaps them waddling along a beach on holiday. Unsightly hairs, beer bellies, botties made blamanche by cellulite – any physical imperfection can be ruthlessly exposed to shatter a famous person's image of supposed beauty. It takes just one picture, usually accompanied by a big neon arrow and screaming headline, to reduce a fantasy figure to the realms of an everyday fatso!

I was once caught off-guard, pictured coming out of a local bookies. I was said to look 'pale' and panicked after an afternoon apparently spent chasing my losses. The truth of the matter was that I'd actually spent an afternoon catching up with a mate and I always look paler in real life than I do on the telly because I don't wear six inches of TV pancake just to leave the house. The photograph was meant to show me worried and clearly not looking my best but in truth it was no worse than the publicity shots they found to adorn the first two series of my show! Launching a brand new host of a brand new show, I thought they'd trawl through the archives to find some nicely touched-up portrait of me looking all gorgeous and manly. I would have had no problem whatsoever with them giving me the full David Cameron and going crazy with the airbrush to show me off to my best advantage, but no. The best they could come up with was a photo of me looking like I'd just gone ten rounds with a bottle of vodka. My eyes were glazed, my face was puffy and I looked absolutely knackered – just like a first-time father. Every time my show went to an advert break my name would flash up on screen next to an image of me that looked like I'd just been turfed out of a casino at six in the morning, still drunk and with no money to get home. Thanks a lot. Oh, the 'glamour' of show business!

Overall though, I have to say that I've been very lucky with the press. As far as embarrassing photos go there's not really a lot they could snap that might shock any of my regular viewers. I mean, I don't go out in my wife's knickers and it surely won't be the greatest surprise in the world for any readers to discover that no, I don't have a Peter Andre six-pack. I'm just as thin and wrinkly on holiday as I am back home so there wouldn't be too much mileage to be had from picturing this particular middle-aged man in his swim shorts! All that aside, I have had one very public ordeal where the cameras I normally feel so comfortable in front of made a terrible experience ten times worse.

A couple of years back I was booked to film something in Doncaster for a DVD. I was being driven up to the location, sharing the back seat of this hulking great BMW with my show's Director of Aftercare, Graham. I'd just been reading how something like 3,000 accidents had occurred on British roads as a result of the lies being told to motorists by satellite navigation systems when I had a first-hand taste of the action myself. I've never liked the condescending know-it-all tone of my own 'Twat-Nav' system and have always resented the way it so frequently sends me the wrong way without so much as an admission of guilt, far less the apology I feel I deserve. This time the system had directed us the wrong way up the A1 before deciding half way along that we should probably make a U-turn and track back the other way for a bit. Typical.

Amir, our driver, went to make the turn suggested by the incompetent computer on board when out of nowhere, the car was speared by another that must have been doing 70 m.p.h easily. We were t-boned completely. The other car rammed straight into Graham, knocking him flying over towards me. I was half asleep at the time and woke to find three airbags exploding in my face and Graham being launched towards my crotch – terrifying in so many ways! What followed next was like an eerie slow motion of what felt like death itself. After the initial thunderous bang of car on car came silence. All around us, white powdery flakes of what looked like snow were coming down, but inside the car! I saw Amir's head hit against the windscreen as I felt two of Graham's ribs crack against my knee. The other car had flipped upside down and careered along the carriageway before finally ending up in a ditch.

Strangely I was initially quite calm in this surreal nether world. I felt lucid, my thoughts coherent. Slightly dazed, Graham and I helped each other out of the car. Miraculously, Amir had only a few scratches on him and we all scrambled away to an embankment. In the distance the other motorist, obviously fine despite his car's smash and somersault, was off, scarpering down the road!

At my feet Amir was pounding the ground in frustration at an accident that could have happened to anyone. Professional pride dented, he was obviously taking this very personally. It was clear this was to be no normal day but it was only after we'd escaped our crumpled cars that things started to take a turn for the truly bizarre.

My first thought was to ring my wife. Unfortunately I broke the golden rule of calling loved ones after an accident. The veneer of calm cracked and instead of saying, 'look, I've been in an accident but everything's all right, there's nothing to worry about' I went with something a tad more hysterical. 'Shit! Shit! Shit! The car's a write-off!" was all I could scream at her between big gulps for breath.

I did nothing to ease her concerns with my jabbering but they were made all the worse when sirens started wailing. People from every emergency service were descending on the scene within what felt like seconds of our smash. And then, from up above, I heard this deafening whirring. It sounded like a scene from *Platoon* as this massive chopper swooped in and set down about fifty yards away. At that point, the ordeal became full-scale farce.

Out of the helicopter jumped three people with these green bibs that had 'BBC Camera Crew' emblazoned across their front and back. While I was trying to take in what had just happened and the weirdness that was now erupting everywhere around us, I had forgotten my wife was on the phone. Hearing the commotion but no longer hearing my voice, she dissolved into a fit of screaming.

I, meanwhile, was stunned into silence by the arrival of this camera crew. What did they want with me? Why would the BBC want to hound me at this of all times? It took me a while to realise that they were not out to 'get me' at all, they were just part of the standard crew for one of those *Traffic Cop* shows. This was their usual helicopter crew, out responding (impressively quickly I might add) to reports of a collision. Alas, with adrenalin having won the day and stupidity now granted complete control of my brain, I decided the time was right to go into hiding. What I needed was a 'detailed, authoritative and extensive' grip on my faculties but as with pre-war Iraq, the only intelligence I could muster was 'limited, sporadic and patchy.' I was suddenly terrified of being caught on camera by a rival channel, so I turned and hot-footed it to a tree a little way up the embankment. What the hell was I thinking? Not a lot . . . I got to the tree and looked back. The excellent emergency services were going about their business but the man who'd hit us was indulging in a bit of filming of his own. He'd decided to come back to the scene and had pulled out his phone and begun filming the two heaps of twisted metal in the road. His video appeared on YouTube about an hour later!

From the safety of my tree I realised what an arse I was being so I started to make my way back down the hill, like a child who'd just been scolded by his mother. 'Stop playing silly buggers, I can see you behind the tree, now get down here immediately!' I still have no idea what came over me, I just knew I didn't want to be filmed by the BBC!

The next stupid thought to plague me was the need to get my suit out of the car. People often get advised to busy themselves at a time of crisis. Well, despite being in the middle of an obvious crisis all I could think about was the fact that I was still busy! I was meant to be filming in a few hours and I didn't want to compound being late by turning up scruffy. Clearly I wasn't thinking straight but to me it seemed perfectly sensible to try and wrench a suit and shirt from the boot of the car.

Not even considering that the car could be a fireball waiting to happen I ambled over in a daze. I was ushered away by a burly fireman who explained the dangers of returning to a petrol-soaked wreck that was leaking fluid all over the road! Some of his colleagues were at the car, checking, searching, trying to make the whole scene safe. Clearly prioritising the need for expediency above the need for me to wear a pressed shirt a little later, they reached into the boot for whatever they were looking for and tossed away the once pristine threads that were no doubt getting in the way. It was at this point I sobbed. Like a proper girl!

Picture it: so-called TV hard man (really, come on, I'm hardly Phil Mitchell!) weeping after seeing one of his shirts thrown on the road. One of my best mates is stood next to me with two cracked ribs, our driver's in bits on the floor, a camera crew are following our every move and I'm having a breakdown because my newly ironed shirt has got a crease in it!

Thankfully it wasn't too long before an ITV people carrier that was also en route to our filming location swooped in to rescue us. I watched with a wry smile as it made the exact same U-turn that had sparked the carnage that was in evidence wherever I looked. I was asked to sign a few autographs for the attending firemen and when that was done I went back to staring into space, trying to take everything in. Shock had really started to seep in now. Thankfully I was spared too much time alone with my own thoughts. Bowling out of the people carrier came big, bald Security John from the show. He scooped us all up in his huge paws and deposited us safely in the back of our new transport. We were soon on our way, discussing the seriousness as well as the ridiculousness of what had just happened as we continued on to Doncaster.

The next morning I awoke, quite sore, to headlines that shouted 'Jeremy Kyle Cheats Death'. I spoke to Graham, who confessed that he'd sobbed himself to sleep the night before, once the enormity of it all had properly dawned on him too. It was clear we had indeed had a very lucky escape. On my phone were about 137 missed calls from concerned well-wishers who'd just seen the papers and wanted to know that we were all OK. One was from my mum, who had left a brilliantly blunt message. 'So, you're not dead then,' was her way of cutting to the quick! Clearly not, Mother, you spoke to me yesterday, a few hours after the crash!

The shock of it hit all three of us at different times and in different ways. All joking aside, it was bloody scary and made all the more confusing by the arrival of what looked like the BBC's equivalent of the *A-Team*. It's safe to say that I was not much up for being filmed that day as anyone who saw my impromptu game of hide-and-seek would surely testify. The whole day's events were bizarre to me – both at the time and even more so on reflection – but they were nothing compared to what I read about the other person involved in our smash that day, the driver of the other car.

At the time, although the YouTube filming and aborted escape down the dual carriageway did strike me as a bit odd, I was just glad that none of us were seriously hurt in the crash. I thought we were all everyday people who had shared in a lucky escape. Imagine my surprise then to read that this man was arrested later after police found five cannabis plants in the back of the car he ploughed into us that day!

It gets worse. My chance encounter with him came on the A1 but it might so easily have happened on my show. Why? Well, it transpired that his forays into horticulture weren't the only matters of interest to the local police. He was arrested a month or so after our crash to discuss everything from cannabis possession and 'abstracting' electricity to common assault and handling stolen goods.

Apparently, in a row with his girlfriend over the naming of their child, he had pushed her into a canal before laughing and filming it! This thirty-six-year-old man even told officers that he didn't think it mattered too much because she was 'already wet from the rain'! The police made their move and carted him off in one of their cars for questioning. It was at this point, on the same stretch of road he'd flipped his own car via ours and a couple of Graham's ribs, that he tried to escape. While the police car was doing sixty-five miles an hour! He kicked out at the officers in the car with him, cracked the windscreen and yanked at the wheel in an attempt to drag the car back to that ditch he must have now felt so bonded to. His plan was to have another high-speed crash in order to escape from the police! Madness.

It goes without saying that if he had been on my show and I'd been made aware of all this, I would have been giving him both barrels whilst telling his missus that she could do a whole lot better. And do you know what, I wouldn't have cared how many cameras filmed me saying it! As it was, this strange tale unfolded not too far from the Nottinghamshire town of Newark, which is an anagram of the most fitting word I can think of to describe this man . . .

Possession of drugs, fiddling the electricity meter, pushing his girlfriend in a canal, handling a stolen laptop and then trying to break out of a speeding police car doing over sixty along the same road he'd nearly killed himself and us on a few weeks earlier – what an absolute 'Newark' indeed.

11

You've Changed!

Kirk Douglas once said that fame does not so much change *you* as everyone else around you. I think he might have a point. Ever since landing myself a job on television I have sensed a waiting, in some cases maybe even a longing, for me to disappear up my own backside. It seems that certain friends, family and colleagues are desperate for that moment when they can say, 'yes, Jeremy's changed – I always knew he would.'

Being tired, a tiny bit irritable or even just a little fed up is no longer an option for me anywhere but at home, where my wife and three young children rarely cater for such luxuries anyway. If, for example, a delivery does not turn up at the allotted time I have paid for, I cannot complain. If I feel I am being ripped off by anyone selling me gas or electricity I can do little more than smile sweetly and thank them as they shaft me. If I were to suggest for just one second that some thieving oiks were unfairly diddling me, I'd be accused of being an unreasonable jumped up little diva!

It won't surprise anyone to learn that I am not backwards in coming forwards when I think that standards could be better. I have always stood up for my rights when I think

85

I'm being stitched up. It therefore came as quite a shock to the system when it transpired that a genuine complaint, fairly made I thought, had been reworked to read as me throwing a celebrity tantrum.

The fact is that one overheard phone conversation, no matter how innocent, is all it takes for someone to have a story on you. One misplaced word or slip of the tongue is all someone needs to call the *Sun* with 'proof' that you have been spotted, and spotted being an asshole! I learned my lesson after I was observed speaking my mind about bad service in a well-known suit hire shop. The next day it was reported that I had 'lost it' (I hadn't) and exploded with rage (I didn't) whilst unfairly berating a 'poor, terrified shop assistant' (he wasn't).

What actually happened was that the suit I'd hired wasn't there as promised. The guy serving was overworked so I helped unload their lorry and drag in some more stock for the other equally worried customers who were similarly not going to be able to meet their function's dress code. I will admit to having been a bit narked when there was no suitable suit on the lorry I'd just helped unload, but there was no great hissy fit. I knew my kids would be restless in the car outside and the situation was annoying, so I guess I reacted as I always had done in days gone by when things I'd paid for hadn't come up to scratch. The thing is, under the terms of the unspoken, invisible contract I have apparently signed, this is no longer allowed and my justifiable irritation was misrepresented as unwarranted fury in the press the next day. Oops!

That first taste of life after a quick lick of fame was enough to change my behaviour: I'm pretty careful when I'm out and about these days. The small amount of fame I'm currently enjoying might have changed some things about me but one thing is for certain, it has, as Kirk Douglas suggested, changed a hell of a lot in almost everyone around me.

Some friends, and even family, have sold stories, others have made up lies about me, manipulated and blackmailed me and a few I thought would be the closest of allies were actually at the head of the queue to betray me for money. As a result, I have been forced to re-evaluate lifelong bonds, which I find very painful.

And for all the support I am grateful to receive from so many loyal viewers of my show, there are some whose stated intention is to actually do me serious harm. I have had threats to bomb the studios where I work, I've been pelted with bricks whilst trying to film in the street and I've received a few letters promising to kill me and my family. One time my wife rang me in tears after a car full of menacing strangers swung into our drive demanding to see 'that Jeremy Kyle!' Who were they? What did they want? What would they have done if I had been in? Will they come back? These are terrifying thoughts for a father away from his wife and three babies.

The change in circumstances that comes with a little bit of fame means that inevitably, your outlook changes. For me, for a time, paranoia set in. Read enough death threats and know that thugs are turning up and scaring your family and I bet you'd find it hard to maintain normality too. The paranoia subsides but you're not the same as you were.

Most change is not that big a deal. The more sinister things are, although petrifying, thankfully quite few and far between. More immediate and more predictable, I suppose, are the changes in attitude that seep into people who stop seeing you as a friend and start treating you as their own personal cash cow. People who before made a virtue of proudly paying their own way have come out of the woodwork to demand I-O-Us they haven't paid back and barely even thanked me for. Sometimes you hear it said that famous people feel entitled to this or that but I have to say that the minute my mug was on the telly, a lot of people seemed to think that *they* were entitled to a piece of me. It was like they assumed I must suddenly be a multimillionaire and they wanted as many cups of cash as they could carry from the money tap they figured was newly installed at the bottom of my garden.

I remember I once tried to help a man I considered the closest of friends. His life was a mess, his relationship in tatters and he had suffered a terrible bereavement. He was in tears on my doorstep and as he was a friend I'd always promised I'd do anything for, I arranged a £5,000 loan for him. He took it, but to this day I have not heard from him. My money, but more importantly our friendship, vanished into thin air.

That was my first real taste of the sucker punch that can knock you out when real friends change as a result of your success. Naively, I guess I always thought friends would simply be happy to share in and celebrate each other's triumphs. I've always been chuffed to bits to see my mates do well but that hasn't always been the case the other way round. To lose the warmth, sincerity and honesty that used to bond you so tightly to those you loved is horrible but it has happened a lot to me – and various friends of mine who are also in the public eye. As a result I think I have probably become more wary. How could I not?

As I said, I've had to make all sorts of changes to my lifestyle. For me at least, career-ending traps and potential tabloid scandal lurk around every corner. I mean, I couldn't very well preach the need for my guests to drink responsibly if I was out getting blitzed in every pub in town. Imagine if I were splashed across the papers crashing drunkenly out of bars on to the street, a bit like some of the *Loose Women* – I'd be sacked on the spot! Thankfully I'm a lightweight. I don't miss going out and besides, I need to get home to my family but even so, turn down enough friendly invites to join people for a drink after work and the suspicion will be that 'you've changed' and can no longer be bothered. The truth is if I fancy a drink I'll now more than likely have one at home or in a quiet restaurant. The only change there is of a man who has gone from thirty-nine to forty-four years old and has had two more babies to add to his brood.

My life at home has kept me as busy and grounded as I was before telly – three children aged six and under are no respecters of fame, trust me! The hectic work schedule also keeps me fairly distracted from the stresses that consume the bigger egos of the celebrity world. I try not to get too involved in backbiting and petty jealousies and I don't go in for the wilder demands that I've heard some very well known faces are prone to. I don't need sixteen lilies in my dressing room and petals scattered wherever I walk. A cup of coffee will do. Well OK, an airy-fairy media latte is what I actually order and preferably in a china cup. D'oh, what have I become!

So, how can I avoid disappearing up my own backside? To be fair, it's tougher than you might think. I agree that being famous grants me privilege, status and opportunity far beyond anything I am morally entitled to, and the danger is that once you feel entitled to all that, the necessary narcissism that lies within most performers is liable to run out of control.

When I first joined ITV I knew nobody. It was everybody's job to make the new guy feel welcome so that I would be relaxed enough to do my job. People fell over themselves to offer me coffees and comforts at every turn, and I quickly got used to them. In TV-Land very few people are honest enough to tell a presenter when they've been less than impressive. Instead they fluff and faff and paint pretty pictures of the world and your place in it lest your fragile confidence be crushed and you can't perform for the cameras. (That makes it sound a bit porno. The fluffing is all verbal, the stroking all metaphorical and only of ego, nothing else!) But basically, everyone tells you how great you are, how wonderfully well you did and how fantastic everything is going to be now *you* are at the helm. With very few exceptions people queued up to dish out praise when I first arrived. I'm not saying I earned all of it or even that I believed it. The point is I kept hearing it, and to have praise lavished upon you and to be indulged with loveliness all the time, by talented, perpetually smiling people can be dangerous. It can start the blowing of the smoke up a man's bottom that might overly inflate that man's ego!

What at first feels like having an undeserved army of butlers at your beck and call gradually becomes the norm. And when it becomes the norm it can then start to feel like your – danger! danger! – right. Your divine entitlement, yours, yours, yours! It sounds horrible to say it but it is true, and it would be true of anyone reading this, given enough time.

I am no less grateful to have my shirts pressed, my suits bought and clothes all laid out for me now than I was a thousand shows ago but I confess the wide-eyed wonder of it all has faded. I know that's what happens on a show day and I have now been conditioned to expect it. In fact, it throws me off kilter if it's not done! I remind myself to say thank you to everyone, every day, in make-up, wardrobe and everywhere else but now I am used to them, and they are used to me, the familiarity that breeds contempt can set in. From both sides. One bad mood from me though, one missed 'thank you' and I might well be considered to be showing signs of becoming an over-indulged monster, too big for his boots. One demand, one sandwich I don't like, one coffee I don't drink and I might now be said to have changed, just like they 'always knew I would!'

12

What Do Girls Want?

Once, I was out in the car with my teenage daughter when a man drove up next to us at the lights, wound down his window and screamed at me, 'Oi Kyle, you're a C*NT!' I was naturally taken aback and wondered how this rabid, frothing, seething little idiot's rage might next manifest itself. I wanted to say something but I did not. I could not, for all the reasons I've mentioned in the previous chapter. I remained impassive, waited an eternity for the lights to change and pulled away slowly as Rent-a-yob screeched off into the distance.

Once he'd gone I felt anger but also a sort of impotence. There's a feeling a lot of blokes will recognise – that of regretting having done nothing when challenged aggressively, having reacted too late to do anything differently. Imagine being confronted by a mouthy idiot in a bar, say, and not responding as you would have wished in all your past macho dreams. The quick quip to diffuse the situation never materialises, the Jackie Chan gumption to stand up to a physical challenge temporarily goes AWOL. Once the immediate threat has passed, feelings of 'I coulda-woulda-shoulda done that' often flood the male psyche, mocking a very public loss of face and manliness. My brief confrontation at the lights left me feeling exactly like that. And my sense of emasculation was made all the worse because the incident took place in front of my teenage daughter, who was none too impressed with the lack of balls displayed by her Old Man that day!

Hattie watched in disbelief as the abuse poured through our window. I stayed silent, and shrivelled in my seat. The warnings of a thousand TV bosses echoed through my head and the natural urge to respond was dulled in me by a professional obligation not to. My daughter looked down at me, disgusted. I think she called me a 'pussy' as she questioned how Kyle family honour could go so pathetically undefended.

The reason for my silence is that I have achieved what 73 out of 100 recently surveyed school children said was all they wanted for themselves in later life: fame. As a (fairly) famous man I can't voice displeasure in public even though, ironically enough, that is what I am in-part paid to do at work. 'Kicking off' (something I'm definitely not paid to do), even in the face of overwhelming provocation, would end up in the papers and my reputation could be damaged to the point where the career that feeds all my family's dreams is jeopardised. It's a funny old world.

I was initially horrified to hear that seventy-three per cent of all British children just wanted to be famous. Whatever happened to being the best, the most talented? Or wanting to help others? Where are all the wannabe nurses and young vets of tomorrow? Even those who want to achieve fame as an actress or the next pop princess should surely at least have some drive to master an art first – be it singing, acting or dancing. What have we come to when so many of our children see being famous as the only goal? How can being the next contestant on *Big Brother* be just as desirable as being the next Madonna?

As I say, initially I was appalled but thinking about it from their point of view, who can blame them? The riches and rewards of being famous are played up for all to see. There's no balance though. It's all sequins and stardust with too few people pointing out that true talent and a lot of hard work is required for the select few who make it. In the absence of this key message though, is it any wonder our kids have become so confused? Magazines tell impressionable young girls to be thin and beautiful to the exclusion of all else. Too many girls' heads are being filled with the idea that all they need to do is stay fit, well-groomed and scantily clad – do that for long enough at the right bar in town and you could be the next WAG! Cavort around on a reality show with next to nothing on and you might get to live the life of a Russian oligarch, better still you might even bag one!

It really does worry me that we've gone so far with the whole celebrity obsession and now we risk losing too many of our next generation, blinded by hollow dreams they might never achieve, with no Plan B to fall back on. How can we have got to the stage where fame in and of itself is the sole ambition? If my children came to me and said that all they wanted to be is famous, I'd think I'd failed as a parent. Seventy-three per cent of children do think that though, and they are just the tip of the iceberg. They have bought wholesale into a celebrity culture of which they see little more than glittery sugarcoated slices via the *X-Factor*. But what future for them – and for all of us – if that is really the case? Where is the country sliding?

I recently heard of TV's Dr Linda Papadopoulos talk of another survey in which one thousand British girls were also asked that age-old favourite: 'what do you want to be when you grow up?' I was shocked, truly shocked, to learn that the top answer, with sixty per cent, was *glamour model*! Second, and even more shockingly, twenty-five per cent of all girls surveyed said they wanted to be a *lap dancer*! I am a father of three daughters and it staggers me to think there might be an eighty-five per cent chance that any of them would harbour career ambitions that never went beyond toplessness! That just can't be right in this day and age – we've surely got to want and demand more of our daughters.

I'm not out to run down anyone engaged in either of those professions. I know there are a lot of women who do so happily and very profitably. I'm sure there's quite a few canny businesswomen among the glamour modelling and lap dancing set, ladies who make the most of their assets in order to make as much money as possible in as short a space of time before getting out and setting up in business elsewhere. The smart cookies, the really intelligent and savvy girls who decide to go into those professions quite coldly, are the ones who use the fully rounded and developed flesh inside their skulls, not the stuff stuck on front of their chests!

There's no getting around it though, sixty per cent is just way too high a ratio of young girls wanting to pursue some-thing as shallow as glamour modelling. Too many will be too naive and, if this is all they want to do, too under-qualified elsewhere, to make sound judgements – either in the industry, or more probably on the outside of it, if and when things go wrong.

Where are the back-up plans? Where's the emphasis on education? I can almost understand a smart PhD student wrapping her body round a pole each night to relieve some drunk men she couldn't care less about of the money she needs to pay for her education. What concerns me though is that too many young girls are getting too hung up on the idea of selling their sex at too early an age to ever really give themselves a chance of developing their potential in all the other areas of life they should be grasping. If girls are growing up needing men's sexual approval in order to feel happy and self-confident, what hope is there? They are setting them-selves up for the most horrible and crushing of falls.

As Dr Papadopoulos highlighted too, this sexualisation of girls from way too young is negatively impacting on other areas of society too. At the very top of the money pile, young women are seeing it as acceptable, cool even, to be passed around a premiership football team like some piece of meat in the hope that one player might take a long-term shine to them. Some girls do just that, in the hope of hitting their version of the big time – laying on their backs like little more than hookers, waiting for the next present, tip, day out shop-ping or child support payment!

A friend's young sister once said to me that she wouldn't consider snogging anyone in a nightclub unless they were wearing an 'Armani suit – minimum!' That was about six years ago and things have got progressively worse. Whole packs of girls now go out hunting for men with money. Finding one, being his plaything and getting pregnant really does seem to be the only ambition some have. I have given a few girls on my show quite a hard time for wanting nothing more than to get pregnant so as to get a council house. I stand by that, but it is really no worse than a girl sneaking out from Mummy and Daddy's house in the suburbs and trying to get pregnant by anyone rich or famous who might then pay all the bills so they never have to work! The common denominator is apathy. There is a lack of desire to work hard and use their brains to really make something of themselves. That leads to warped ambitions and questionable morals, with young girls thinking first of their sex as a means of getting ahead. That has to be wrong.

I don't want to be a hypocrite here. While I have never been a lap dancer and can't ever quite see myself cutting it as a glamour model, I do understand why some people want to be famous. They are only signing up to what they see as a quick route to a carefree lifestyle of fun and fast cars that might always be denied them by more traditional careers. I get that, I really do but people who buy *only* into that are seeing only the icing on top of a very large cake, and not the ingredients of the cake itself.

The job I have and the life it has given me and my family is far beyond the wildest dreams I ever had as a student carousing his way through university. I will never turn into someone who takes the money, has the good time and then moans about how terrible it is to be in the public eye. I can't stand those people who seemingly have it all but still carp on about the 'terrible price' of fame. I certainly will not be doing so here.

I've already acknowledged that there are a few restrictions (no speaking your mind about poor service or when some idiot has a go at you!) and there are risks involved with making a private life into public property. That said, they are quite easy to manage in the grand scheme of things. If you don't want to be reported as a naughty boy, don't be a naughty boy. If it is going to be a little bit embarrassing to explain to your children why you were found tied up by ten hookers with an orange in your mouth and a banana up your bum, it's probably best to give all that a miss!

In show business especially, fame and the life that comes with it is easily lost. It is fickle and can be snatched away almost overnight. If you want the media to stay interested in you, it is surely best to offer something more than just teeth and tits. And bad news for those eighty-five per cent of girls surveyed: all of the truly talented female stars have teeth and tits too!

For myself, I know that if ever I find my privacy invaded or profile elevated to a level my family can no longer endure, I can hang up my microphone and walk away, safe in the knowledge that I could return to a successful career in sales and business. Life would be returned to 'normal' for all of us pretty damn soon. The fact that I choose not to, and, moreover, the reason that all the moaners don't either is that there are so many life-enriching opportunities available to people who make their living in the public eye. I can't deny them nor knock anyone who thinks they look more appealing than their present lot. What worries me is the means too many of our country's future young ladies might think best to achieve them.

I'm going to sound a warning. If all you care about is being 'famous', you could be on a dangerous path. For everything you can gain superficially and materially, fame can also drain so many of the things that money can never buy. Develop a skill, hone a talent and work hard with the support of those who will always keep you grounded. If fame follows, by virtue of your success being celebrated, good. But if it is fame for fame's sake you seek, what you ultimately achieve might not turn out to be all it seemed in the tabloid brochure. And that goes for boys as well as girls . . .

13

Facebook? I Might Just Poke it!

Psst! Guess what? I'm not a big fan of Facebook. Now I know we're all 'friends' here so you won't go and tell anyone, will you? You'll keep that little admission just between us – best friends forever – right? Yeah, *right* more like!

To be honest I can't help but laugh out loud, sorry LOL, at the stupidity of people who think that a juicy private post on Facebook will never make its way back to the one person they didn't want to hear it. I wouldn't tell my top twenty friends something that needed to be kept secret, far less a hundred. Why take the risk? Titbits of gossip can shoot around an office in seconds so it stands to reason that anything sensational or salacious won't stay quiet for long if you whisper it into the online ears of hundreds of people, friends or not. And besides, who out there genuinely has 135 friends (apparently the average for a Facebook user) they can truly trust with the most intimate details of their private life?

Take the Crystal Palace footballer who scuppered his career by prematurely announcing that his 'dream move' to the Premiership was imminent. Ashley-Paul Robinson got a little ahead of himself when he updated his Facebook profile status to reveal to 2.7 million other users that he was 'goin Fulham Monday' and that 'if I pull dis off I'm on dis ting'!

To be fair he didn't mean to send it to 2.7 million people, that was a mistake. He had only intended to send the message to 198 friends but even so, did he really think that news like that would stay quiet? It only takes one gossipy friend or fiercely loyal football fan to spill the beans, so why risk it? In this case it was the football fans that began chirping first and news of Ashley-Paul's desire to defect from one team to the other became a topic of hot debate. As it turned out he failed to impress at his trial with Fulham but the whole sorry saga had so displeased his employers at Palace that they dumped him! Ashley-Paul's is a case in point, a microcosm of the sorts of problems that mass verbal diarrhoea spewed on to the pages of Facebook are causing.

I meet so many people who have been the author of their own downfall, via Facebook. More and more guests on my show are basing their accusations on things they've read on one of their 'friend's' Facebook pages. Obviously in my line of work, it tends to be unintended confessions of infidelity. I have lost count of the number of people who first had their suspicions aroused by the amount of time their partner spent on Facebook. I frankly find it incredible that so many people unwittingly, or sometimes even deliberately, admit to straying without considering that their other half might, just might find out. Some are so obvious about it they make John Terry look discrete! And it is not just on my show. Out in the wider world, Facebook is the cause or catalyst behind break-ups everywhere.

At the time of writing, Facebook has an active usership of about 350 million people. If Facebook were a country it would have the third largest population of any nation in the world, bigger than the United States and behind only China and India. Interestingly, it is reckoned that sixty per cent of Facebook users have either looked up or are back in touch with ex-lovers. Now I'm not saying there is anything wrong in that necessarily. It is lovely when old flames can carry on as just good friends once their relationship has ended. Similarly there needn't be anything particularly untoward with looking up an ex via the internet, just to check in, say hi and see how the years have treated them. Nostalgia and innocent curiosity aside though, it is impossible to ignore the potential for extramarital naughtiness when roughly 210 million people are in touch with the true loves of yesteryear! I'm sure in some cases the reuniting of childhood sweet-hearts can be quite endearing but all too often such a recon-nection comes at the expense of the partner and family presently in tow.

On my show it happens all the time. People bury their heads in the cybersand and get quickly involved in intense online relationships that take up all the time they should be spending on the ones they've got in real life. People hide from the difficulties they're experiencing with their partners, then talk them through with 'friends' online instead of confronting the issues head on with the person concerned.

Of course none of this is Facebook's fault. If a person is going to cheat they will do so regardless of whether or not they have a social networking account. Similarly, Facebook in itself can't destroy a relationship. Granted, it may make things worse but it can't manufacture the unhappiness in the first place. The partners who stray, the people who face-book (yes it's a verb now too) excessively and those who use it as a permanent shop window on all the other loves they might still have (or have back!) must bear the responsibility for the actions they take. That said, the facility Facebook provides does seem to be luring more and more into a temptation they cannot resist. I noticed the rise on my own show but I am not alone. A leading British law firm came to the same conclusion in 2009, pointing to the fact that twenty per cent of their new petitions for divorce contain some reference to Facebook.

It is a sad indictment of our times that the site has also become a tool for bullying. Guests on my show have frequently accused others of spreading lies about them via Facebook, of stirring trouble and even co-ordinating campaigns of intimidation. I remember only too well being terrified of the bully in the school playground and the panic and isolation that could quickly swallow up anyone who fell foul of the mobs that ruled during 'playtime'. Those familiar fears and feelings of intimidation have been described to me on the show, only now the threats often originate on the pages of Facebook. This harassment is definitely on the rise so I was glad to see the precedent set in 2009, when the first three-month sentence was handed out to a nasty piece of work who had threatened to kill a teenager she'd first begun bullying at school some three years earlier. I don't believe that this will be the last sentence of its kind. Not by a long chalk.

Despite all the bad behaviour of some of its users, I'm not really anti-Facebook. Granted, I can't quite fathom why certain idiots want to compromise themselves by revealing *every*thing but at the end of the day that's their look out. I don't understand the need to detail your every thought, movement or bodily function either. I mean really, who cares? I don't want to know what you've just had for dinner, what you fancy for tea, and whether or not you're for or against Jordan (I was always Team Andre, not that I expect you to care!). I find it all a bit pointless but maybe that's just my age talking; in fairness I don't understand any music more modern than ABBA either! Anyway, given all the people I meet who definitely *are* out getting up to no good at all hours of the day and night, I suppose I should be grateful for those whose only contribution to municipal mayhem is confined to forwarding the latest funny from YouTube.

And, as I always say, there are two sides to every story ... Lots of people sing Facebook's praises – recently even the police. Or, more particularly, a lady who turned 'Facebook Detective' in order to bring her attacker to justice.

Jennifer Wilson was rammed in the face with a pint glass whilst out clubbing one night. She vaguely recognised one of the assailant's friends from Facebook so she searched online for him. She found him and then via his profile searched about 200 other profile pages until she found the guy who'd assaulted her that night. Armed with the picture and, one would have thought, all the information needed for the police to act, she went down to her local station. Amazingly they sent her away to do some more digging – they wanted Jennifer to come back and tell them where her attacker worked! Stunned to be asked but determined to see the job through, she got the information and watched justice prevail as her enemy from that night went down for 120 hours community service. Jennifer was also awarded £2,400 in damages that would never have been hers were it not for the existence of Facebook.

I suppose, thinking about it, there is a lot we can *all* be grateful to Facebook for, and all the other sites like it. It is of course a superb way of getting in touch with loved ones. Lost families have been found, old friendships – and not just those that end up in the bedroom – have been rekindled. People scattered to all four corners of the planet now have a means of caring, sharing and remaining bonded. I applaud that, and all the potential positives the Facebooks of this world give us but I do still find the prospect of logging on to stay in touch a little impersonal. A message to a Facebook page will never really replace even the briefest of phone calls for me. A few minutes of actually hearing someone's voice will always mean more to me than some snatched sentences bashed out and boshed down the line for me to read on my laptop.

In fact, I still mourn the demise of traditional 'snail mail'. I'll never be able to properly convey to my kids the thrill that once came with opening a letter I'd waited for days to receive from a loved one. If I suggested my oldest daughter send an actual letter home to her grandparents she'd probably think I was mad but I think all kids should now be taught to do it at school. Formal letter writing, sure, but even the young ones should be made to scribble something out and send it off from time to time, as part of a class project. Imagine the look on granny's face when she gets a surprise letter from her favourite grandson. Imagine the lift it would bring to her day to get something like that out of the blue. It would be brilliant and lovely and warm and good. Let's get it done.

Overall, even I can concede that the immediacy of modern communication is 'better'. Certainly, no one can deny that is infinitely more efficient but for me, an email or worse, a bloody Facebook poke, will never have the same romantic impact as a good old-fashioned handwritten letter! Similarly, nothing synthesised in the virtual world will ever replace real encounters with my friends. I don't see how it could. For instance, I watched someone in my office receive a virtual pint sent from a friend of his who lived up the road. A virtual pint? Sent to a Facebook page? Apparently my colleague 'liked this' and sent a thumbs up to say so. I can't see myself ever getting into that. If you lived on the other side of the world, maybe I'd get the gesture but not when you live up the road. Pick up the phone you tight git, give me a call and we'll meet in the pub for a real pint. Better still I'll buy you one back and we can have a *real* chat in *real* time in the *real* world.

I know that eventually one of my kids will force me to get a grip on the ways and means to really make the most of something like Facebook. I'll probably come late to the party as ever and see the whole thing as a marvel ten years down the line. No doubt as soon as I've got it, everyone else will have moved on to the next big thing and I'll once more be struggling to grasp what is so special about *that* newfangled technology. To be honest, lack of technological nous aside, it'll probably take me about ten years to get through all the Facebook groups that I am told have been set up in my 'honour'.

I was quite touched when my producers first told me we had a following on Facebook. I may even have allowed myself to be a little flattered. Apparently there are about 195 Facebook sites that bear my name in some form. One of them is dedicated to 'Jeremy Kyle Addicts', fans of the show that total more than 70,000 in number. There are a couple of sites (admittedly with only a few followers) that claim I should be Prime Minister and one that says I should go for President. All good, hey? Well, not quite. For every one person who apparently wants me to lead the country there are plenty out there who want it known that I am nothing but a 'knob-head' – 177 people in fact! Moreover, 138 people have signed up to call me 'a mouthy prick' and there are some who are less supportive still. I feel it's only fair to mention the 206 people who claim that they would 'happily torture' me, the three separate sites demanding I be sent to Afghanistan and one that states I am just 'a tool that needs shooting'! Charming.

With all that in mind, you'll understand why I remain content to keep away from Facebook and observe from the sidelines. As far as staying in touch goes, I've only just got used to my BlackBerry and I'm happy enough with that. If people want to talk to me, they can phone. If people want to write, they can email. But if anyone wants to take me for a virtual pint? They can poke it and I'll meet them down the pub for a real one instead!

14

The Day I *Really* Died!

I have always had the greatest admiration for people who make their living proving themselves in front of live audiences night after night. That's probably because deep down I've always wondered if I had it in me to do the same. I could never be a dancer cavorting around in spandex, and crooning isn't an option when you sound like a strangled bagpipe. Since overcoming crippling shyness at school though, I *have* grown quite comfortable performing in front of people but I've always wished that I had what it took to be a genuine stand-up comedian. In this industry there's surely nothing harder than having to stand before a room of a thousand strangers, knowing your only job is to make them laugh, and make them laugh hard. When it goes well, I can't imagine there's much that's more gratifying. Get it wrong though, die on your arse, and I can't think of anything more excruciating. The only time I made a whole room laugh – and for entirely the wrong reasons – was in a hospital, surrounded by a bevy of student nurses.

My time to 'die' happened to occur not long before I literally died, for all of about seven seconds! Looking back on my dual mortification I can easily say which experience hurt the most and it had nothing to do with the burst appendix that first sent me to hospital. No, I was killed by the shame that followed.

Back in the early eighties I had started dating a lovely lady from Zimbabwe called Annie. We had planned a dirty weekend down south, which would involve us borrowing a flat by the seaside and turning it into our very own coastal love shack. Consumed by lusty thoughts, we set off on a bus to Battle (how apt – read on). With most of the rest of me throbbing in anticipation, at first I barely noticed the nagging ache that was slowly knotting the pit of my stomach but it was an ache that got worse with each passing mile and an hour later I was screaming a scream that even the deaf could hear.

Bent double in the bus, sweating and shrieking and writhing in agony, dreams of love had long since yielded to the pain. Eventually the bus driver and his passengers could take no more. The vehicle stopped and we were duly dumped in the middle of Battle. I was not in a good way. All week I'd dreamed of being all close and sweaty and cradled in Annie's arms but not like this! The romantic script was ruined and there was now no other choice: we had to get me to hospital.

Wailing like a banshee and demanding sedation from the strongest drugs known to man, I was deposited at what used to be the Royal East Sussex Hospital. The miracle pain cure I was hoping for did not materialise and I was instead invited to gobble down two paracetamol before making a call and preparing myself for surgery! I rang my mum at 6 p.m. and then called back between yelps at 4 a.m. She informed me calmly that they still hadn't left but would be doing so shortly, obviously after making the obligatory parental picnic and calling round every neighbour in the village to let them know they'd be away for all of twelve hours. By the time they did arrive I was being wheeled towards the operating theatre, babbling like a baby.

When I came to, I was on an all-male ward, full of patients recovering from appendectomies. My surgeon told me that this simple procedure to remove the appendix hadn't been an option for me as mine had popped on the way to theatre. My time under the knife was all about clean-up, flushing out what was left of my appendix and ensuring against potentially fatal infections. They had done what they could and signed off with fifteen stitches sewn into my abdomen and a whacking great hole left gaping in my groin so any remaining poison could be drained away.

After the operation my chest felt really congested and I was always coughing. Each time I coughed, a globule of pus was sneezed down a tube connecting the hole in my groin to a bag by my side. It was absolutely disgusting! Despite looking like a science experiment gone wrong, I was told this was all normal and that I should be right as rain soon enough. All I had to do to get off the ward and back home was make sure I had a poo! Easy. With the amount of crap that seemed to be free-flowing out of my every other orifice, I thought this would be a doddle. If only . . .

Three days I was told it would take and three *weeks* later I was still laid up, with no sign of a knock at that particular door. By this time Annie had gone. Watching bits of her date slowly rot in a bag obviously held little appeal. All I could do, day and night, was cough gunk down a tube and ponder how long it might possibly take for me to produce a turd or two.

By this point I'd made friends and said farewell to scores of old men, all possessed of better bowels than me. I developed a keen sense of toilet envy as one by one they departed for home. With a wave from the end of the ward, I'd go through the same brief conversation at least once a day.

'Bye bye (Bob), you off then?'

'Yes, yes – had a good stiff shit so now I'm off home,' would come the reply. 'You had one yet, Jeremy?'

'No, not yet, pissing like a racehorse though!'

It was the only thing I could contribute to the toiletry chit-chat that was *the* conversational currency of the ward. And it was true. The saline drips I was constantly hooked up to ensured my bladder felt permanently full. I went to the loo every ten minutes but only for number ones, never number twos. I would stand in that urinal thirty times a day and each time I'd be mocked by the sit-down cubicle, vacant across the room.

The full horror of my predicament was soon laid bare to the whole ward, and to *my* full horror, in front of a group of pretty student nurses. Led by a towering shouty doctor, they swung by for their rounds one morning. When it came time to study my notes the good doctor bellowed, 'Ahhhh, Mr Kyle. Mr Kyle here has had an appendectomy! Mr Kyle has had peritonitis! Mr Kyle has had septicaemia, and Mr Kyle is still suffering from bronchil pneumonia!'

Boom boom boom! The diagnoses rang out, like charges in a courtroom, but he saved the worst of my humiliation until the end. Whipping back my sheets he flashed my bits to the world whilst declaring me the only patient there unable to poo! As any man out there will know, a male, ahem, member is not at its most proud when its owner is in pain.

And let me put it this way, I was in a *lot* of pain. He'd revealed the most miniscule eyeful for his attendant gaggle to giggle at.

Not content with merely exposing my (very modest) modesty, he then ordered me to lean to one side and prepare to receive a suppository from one of his charges. And so, half naked in one of those bum-less dressing gowns, I rolled over as asked, to reveal my rump. In doing so though, I leaned on the bag that had been collecting the goo still squirting out of me whenever I coughed. I also dislodged the tube in my groin and what with the extra physical exertion of having to painfully roll around the bed, I began coughing and spluttering like never before. Each time, more poison spewed out of me and on to the mattress. I looked, pleading and panicking into the doctor's eyes, hoping he'd spare me from this awful humiliation. He was undeterred though. My clogged up bowels had clogged up his ward and he insisted that now was the time to get things moving for the both of us again.

He motioned for a student to insert the suppository and she did as she was told. Aggressively. Without so much as a 'hi, how are you?' she rammed this jelly bean right up my backside. There were no pleasantries, no getting to know me, just a thumb being forced where the sun don't shine! The nurse stepped back to admire her handy work but without warning I fired the magic pill right back at her. All of the rolling and writhing around had obviously released some pockets of wind inside me – I could not quite believe what was happening when I unleashed the fart I swear I hadn't a clue had been brewing.

It is a sad irony that the only solid to have passed out of

me in three whole weeks just happened to be the very suppository that was supposed to get things flowing through the departure lounge once more. It was only inside me for a few seconds but it fairly flew back out! Unfortunately it flew straight across the room and headed for the best looking of all the nurses. She ducked, a few more screamed and more than one looked on in complete disgust.

By now my humiliation was complete. I was exposed, with my genitals shrivelled, and pus pumping out of me all over the bed. I was on all fours, arse in the air, fresh from being violated by a nurse's thumb. The only way to end this torment was to escape the ward. The only way to escape the ward was to have a poo. The only way of achieving a poo was to have a laxative shoved up my bum and yet my bum had conspired to spit the bloody thing back out. Right in a poor nurse's face! I felt the whole world was against me, even my own backside!

Thankfully I did eventually return to a more normal means of toileting. Wounds patched up and sealed shut with plastic spray, I was eventually allowed home. A stone and a half lighter and with a walking stick to help me hobble about, I took up residence in my old bedroom at Mum and Dad's. Annie drifted back into my life and with the worst of this saga supposedly behind us we focused anew on a brighter future. We all sat back one Sunday evening to watch Cilla, Bob Carolgees and his awful dog on *Surprise Surprise* when I got the biggest surprise surprise of my life!

A familiar warm, wet and weeping sensation had started to come over me. Again. I looked down beneath my waistband and saw that a familiar foe had made its comeback. My nemesis, the hole in my groin I thought had been sealed, was gaping again. And leaking. Everywhere! I pulled my pants half down in horror and watched them fill with what was heaving out of me. My dad arrived first, but useless as ever, he fainted on the spot. Mother followed with an arm full of towels to wrap me up.

It took two hours to get me to hospital – the ambulance couldn't make it down the road because it was minus seventeen outside! When we eventually arrived it was clear that this time was more serious than the last. I was told later that I died for seven seconds that night. Apparently my insides had not properly healed and my body refilled full of poison. With no vent to escape from it had built and built until it erupted out of the weakest point on my patched-up body – that barely healed hole. It virtually killed me in the process. I had never been to hospital before my appendix first burst but my second visit to fix the same problem meant I wracked up ten weeks out of fourteen stuck on a ward! And most of them were spent desperately willing my bowels into life!

I was in and out of consciousness for long parts of my stays. The drama of what was going on distracted me from the seriousness of the peril I was actually in. Acutely burned in to the fabric of my brain are the horrible episodes that saw me shrink and 'die' with embarrassment. But lost on me until much, much later was the fact that I came so close to actually dying. It took the words of my father to remind me. Ever the bastion of understatement, he gave away nothing at the time. However, in a diary he showed me some years later I came across a written admission that for him was astonishing.

'Been to hospital again this morning. Traffic crap. Nearly lost him today.'

There was no mention of appendix or surgery. There was never a note on my shame with the nurses. Humiliation and emotion didn't come into it but for him this was big – a note in the diary of the day I know I *really* died!

15

Commit an Adult Crime?
Do Some Adult Time!

Nobody was more appalled by the tragic case of Baby P than me. I was writing my first book at the time the whole thing was being played out in the press. I remember the numbness I felt and the shock and revulsion that gripped everyone. It really was a story that seemed to slow time. It forced us all to reflect, with collective shaking of stunned head, how on earth some human beings could stoop so low.

In the wake of that case the spotlight was understandably turned on the failings of some social services. There was a slew of articles that rightly decried the catastrophic over-sights that led to poor Baby P being allowed to remain in the care of such murderous monsters. Anyone who read even the briefest details of the torture Baby P was subjected to would understand the outrage and anger directed towards the professionals that should have saved him. This 17-month-old infant suffered around fifty injuries I still find almost impossible to imagine being beaten into anyone, far less a baby. In the run-up to his death his own mother had stood by and watched as her son was punched in the face so hard that he swallowed one of his baby teeth (later found in Baby P's colon). He was lifted repeatedly by his ears, tearing the skin connecting them to his head, had eight ribs broken and had his spine snapped in what was described in court as part of a campaign by the mum's boyfriend to 'toughen him up'. This baby's back was broken by being forced over a knee or stair banister by some sadistic bastard and yet doctors apparently failed to spot it when examining Baby P! In fact, *sixty* visits by health and care professionals failed to sound the alarm bells that should have saved him.

With this fresh in mind, it would have been easy to assume that all social services were in decline. I wondered myself if the reports I read were just the tip of the iceberg and Baby P might precipitate a series of heart-rending revelations. After all, some eight years earlier and with what was described by a judge as 'blinding incompetence' by social services, another child, Victoria Climbie, had been killed by her carers in the same London borough as Baby P. Thankfully the truth of the matter, according to the latest findings, is quite the opposite. Contrary to popular opinion, social services in this country appear to be good and getting better.

A report shows that the investment we have made in them is bearing considerable fruit. In fact, on balance, Baby P might just come to symbolise the very worst example of an exception that proves the more general rule. The report, produced by Professor Colin Pritchard from Bournemouth University's School of Social Health and Care concluded that violent deaths of children in this country had gone down forty per cent in thirty-five years. In that time England and Wales has gone from having the third and fourth highest rate of child killings in the Western world to the fourth lowest.

This progress has been achieved, most seem to agree, by money being pumped into our social services – money that has been used primarily to recruit more and better social workers.

Of course where the welfare of children is concerned, where even one mistake might cost an innocent life, there can never be any cause for complacency. One life lost that could have been saved will always be unforgiveable so it is a case of working harder and striving to do better until *every* statistic comes back in our children's favour. Credit where credit is due though and a huge pat on the back to the people running a part of the system which we would all have been forgiven for thinking was little more than a shambolic liability.

I am glad to see Great Britain finally moving up a league table it would be good to top. I am obviously pleased that our children seem safer, or at least less in danger of the sorts of deaths that will seem especially unimaginable to anyone who has had any sort of bond with a young child. I congratulate any minister who has fought to stump up the cash that has gone into these departments and it goes without saying that we should all be immensely proud of those overstretched social workers on the ground who all play such a vital role in helping the children and families of the hardest-pressed in this country. Professor Pritchard's report seems to laud them, I loudly applaud them. That said, I do wonder about something that his report does not really go into.

Violent child deaths have gone down but the violence being wrought on children *by* children is getting worse, at least if the headlines are to be believed. In 2008 it was reported that violent youth crime had risen by thirty-seven per cent but, for me, what's even scarier than this rise in kid-on-kid violence is its increasing savagery. I didn't think I would ever be as shocked again as I was wading through the blood-curdling story of Baby P. But then the 'Devil Boys of Doncaster' emerged.

'Beware of the Kids' was the ominous sign that hung on their front door. And most of the community were, so accustomed had they become to being regularly, ritually terrorised by two young brothers aged just eleven and twelve. But nobody could have imagined the almost unutterable violence to which they would subject two other boys, aged eleven and nine. Unprovoked, and apparently carried out just because their attackers were *bored* (?!), two innocent children were subjected to a ninety-minute ordeal which very nearly killed one of them. These 'Devil Boys' engaged in an orgy of depraved violence and sexual degradation that I find hard to believe children can even conceive of, far less see fit to carry out.

The courts heard that these boys forced their victims to strip, before whipping them with sticks, cable and barbed wire. They were pummelled into submission with punches, kicks, bricks, boulders, and one even had a kitchen sink dropped onto his head. The boys were said to be left looking 'chewed up and spat out', like they had gone through 'a masher or mangle' according to one of their parents.

One of the victims managed to scramble away to get help but the other was left fighting for his life, comatose, swollen and blood-caked in a way that reduced the first police officer on the scene to tears. Apparently this boy's last words to his friend, who only managed to escape to get help by pretending to ram a stick down his own throat, were, 'You go and I'll just die here.'

The testimony of all of the witnesses in that case really does challenge the limits of what normal people would think possible but what I have described is undoubtedly true. In fact a large part of the attack was filmed by one of the brothers, who claimed at the time it might make 'one hell of a picture'.

The picture created in my mind is plenty hellish enough but it is one made all the more so by the sentences which were handed out to these two young sadists. Minimum detention terms of five years each were considered just by the judge. I think them the very height of unjust leniency. Have we learned nothing from the case of Jon Venables – back in prison after too little time behind bars for his part in the savage murder of toddler, James Bulger?

I understand the lobby who claim with some justification that the 'Devil Boys' are victims too. Brought up by a waste-of-space mother who allegedly drugged their food when she wanted 'a quiet night', theirs was a life dominated by drugs and extreme violence from the moment they were born. They were beaten regularly, as was their mother – who also had five other children by two other dads – and growing up they could smoke, booze and watch violent or pornographic films at will.

It is perhaps no surprise that these kids went off the rails so spectacularly but the desperately unfortunate nature of their predicament neither diminishes nor excuses their responsibilities. For their victims' sakes *and* for their own sakes, being detained for five years just isn't enough. They have had a life of appalling neglect that has led them at the ages of just eleven and twelve to commit crimes I suggest should see any adult convicted of the same locked up for life. These boys could be out around their sixteenth birthdays and even those who plead mitigating cicumstances must surely suspect that if we let them out so soon, they are bound to offend again – and who knows how much worse the consequences might be next time? No, they need to be locked away for a very long time. In a place more safe, stable and secure than any they have yet known, they should be made to sit every rehabilitation course going over a period of at least ten years and then we should review the situation. By then they'll still only be twenty-one/twenty-two but at least after a decade minimum we might be able to properly assess if anyone's been successful in repairing some of the damage done to these boys. Moreover, unlike with Jon Venables, we will have worked on them into their adult years and will be better able to assess whether or not as young adults there is any hope for them in a decent, civilised society.

Ten years is the very least their victims deserve too, although I'd bet that even that would not feel like nearly enough to them or their families. If my children had been tortured in this way I cannot see that I would ever come to a rational conclusion of reasonable punishment. I'd be blinded by fury and a pain that might very well push me into thinking that locking them up for life in solitary confinement was the most lenient sentence I'd ever accept.

Essentially, I believe the normal rules of dealing with children have to be abandoned when the children themselves abandon normal, decent – and child-like – behaviour. Background and upbringing shouldn't come into it nearly as much as history of violence and the potential for reoffending. Society deserves protection from *anyone* capable of committing sick, violent acts on another person, regardless of their age. If any child commits the sort of crime normally the preserve of only the most deranged and despicable adult, they should be treated the same as that adult in order to protect the rest of us. I think that in most cases the crime should be judged every bit as harshly as the criminal.

Take another case, of a thirteen-year-old rapist who received only a three-year sentence for forcing sex on a girl he'd threatened to kill if she did not comply. After the attack, he also stole her iPod and mobile phone. He later even bragged of the assault to the girl's boyfriend on that same phone!

Now, you will never convince me that three years is enough for that boy to either get rehabilitated or reflect properly on his actions from the confines of a cell. It certainly wouldn't come close for the victim. Even the eight years prescribed for adult rapists in similar cases wouldn't come close. Some very tolerant parents out there might seek leniency on the basis of his age. 'He's too young to properly understand the consequences of his actions,' they might bleat. They might take a rather different view if he was a neighbour. Say they had a teenage daughter, how would they react to knowing this boy was coming back to live next door, and at just the age when teenage boys traditionally start to get ever more interested in sex? I bet a three-year sentence under those terms would seem distressingly light!

Knowing right from wrong is surely in us from an early age. Even those brothers from Doncaster will have known that the assaults, intimidation and bullying they were regularly getting away with before they committed their worst atrocities – which anyone alive can't fail to know were as criminally wicked as ever can be – were wrong. Police, teachers and social services stepped in thirty-one times to censure the boys though sadly, again, without ever managing to actually stop them. Even if they got no guidance at home, the tellings-off at school and the general revulsion most people must have shown them whenever they behaved so disgustingly would have reinforced even a rudimentary sense of right and wrong. Knowing it, recognising it and then choosing to violently ignore it for one's own gratification should in my view be punished equally, irrespective of age. If one human being can so brutally strip another of so much dignity, security and freedom they have to be dealt with properly, severely – from eight to eighty.

I have long held firm to my suspicion that some people are just evil. In some cases I'll concede it seems as though that evil is thrust upon someone who had little real hope of avoiding it. However tragic that reality, the simple fact remains that it is more important to protect the rest of society from evil for as long as it remains a danger to them. No exceptions, no excuses and no get out of jail free cards given out on the basis of age alone!

16

Is She Ava'n a Laugh?

Show me a parent who doesn't think that *their* children are the most beautiful examples of procreation in history and I'll show you a liar. I guarantee that even the anti-breeders, those who complain that their mates have been blinded by love when they bang on about the perfection of a newborn that looks 'just like any other baby' will transform the instant they cradle their own child in their arms. No matter the tantrums to follow, or even the amount of milky vomit daily churned up onto your favourite clothes, if *you* are gazing down upon *your* baby, there is nothing in this world that will convince you that any other child ever born could ever have been more gorgeous.

I am no different. And I'm sorry to every other parent on the planet but you are all wrong, every single one of you. You are wrong, I am right and all the rest of you are only ever going to be playing for second place: my children are the most beautiful in the world. Bar none. No exceptions. End of.

Anyway, knowing that they are beautiful is one thing. Actually getting to know them is something completely different. You might think it fairly safe to assume that a child would be made up of a mix of the characteristics brought to the table by its parents. The parents supply the material that comprises any baby's genetic code and the two people a child spends most time with are mummy and daddy, at least in most families like mine. Now, I know my wife inside out, likewise her with me and between us we can see exactly which traits our young brood are inheriting from each of us. All except one, that is!

Alice, our six-year-old, is the perfect example of how I always thought young children would absorb and represent the personalities of both parents. She is the absolute embodiment of Carla and me. I call her 'mini-Mummy' as a result of her endless singing and dancing. Alice is brilliantly sweet, the sort of girl I can see one day pestering me to go to stage school or drama class or, worse, on *The X-Factor*! She sings all the time and is forever starring in her own Command performance of whatever we are doing that day. She gives love and affection ceaselessly, is always hugging us, kissing us, inviting us to play or just showing us how everyone should enjoy life. She is energetic and flighty and loves to dress up – just like her mother. She also, bless her, shows an occasional inability to deal with some of the emotions that get the better of us all in life – just like me! Alice will have the most wonderful life and the whole world will be her stage on which to play. She will smile and charm her way into a great many hearts but, alas, may be one of those whose adorability is preyed upon by the odd bastard among the male half of the population. She'll always be loved and she will one day find true happiness but I fear she'll probably get her heart broken a fair few times along the way. God help her, and God help *him* when those times come!

Henry is still just a baby – nine months old at the time of writing – but even so he is starting to, perhaps worryingly, exhibit a fair few characteristics of his Old Man. Half a lifetime ago, when I was sashaying my way through university, I may have been prone to the odd excited grin whenever a pretty female student walked into the room. I have to say Henry is the same, even now, and with any lady who comes over to coo at him. He is the most mild-mannered, temperate and good-natured of children. Never stressed, always happy – he's every inch the bouncing baby boy but for some reason he just gets that little bit more excited whenever a woman's around. He might as well have Britney's 'Womanizer' as his theme tune. I'm going to have to watch him when his loins start talking, like only they can to a teenage boy!

He has recently developed a habit of nuzzling any nubile stranger to whom he is introduced. His 'M.O.' is to lure young ladies to him by beaming brightly and burbling sweet nothings. Seduced by his charm, said young lady will typically sweep in for a cuddle, whereupon Henry wastes no time at all in burying his head right between her boobs! I have no idea where he gets that from (a-hem) but he's definitely a Kyle lad, that's for sure. In fact, thinking about it, he has more than a touch of my own Old Man about him, the randy old goat!

The exception in our family, the person who so beautifully and uniquely confounds our every expectation is the one, the only: Ava Elizabeth Kyle. She is just four years old but already she's stamped an indelible mark on us, and I reckon she'll carry on to compel the whole world. If my Alice is likely to endure a few broken hearts while finding her way to true love, Ava will undoubtedly be the heart-breaker. If ever we're called upon to mop up Alice's tears as some boy or other proves himself unworthy, I guarantee that at the same time, queuing round the block, will be a line of suitors all forlornly hopeful of finding favour with Ava.

'Finding Favour With Ava.' It could be a movie title. It sums up her first four years on Planet Earth, or, more accu-rately, the rest of the world's first four years on Planet Ava. I'll be blunt: the thing about Ava is that she just does not give a shit. She could not care less about what you say to her, think of her or the way you act around her. She has resolved to deal with the world on her terms and she is a marvel to behold. From Day One, Carla always told me that she would be stunning, and she is. But I'm not talking about simple good looks, although she has those in abundance. For me, the most remarkable thing is her coolness, her determi-nation to be detached and not conform like the rest of us lemmings. She never seeks to impress or out-do anyone to get attention or reward, she just goes about her business and watches everyone come to her – and that's when the fun really starts.

I could not for one minute tell you where she gets this strength, independence or, indeed, capacity for immediate excellence in all she does. I'd love to take the credit but I can't. Where Alice is all stardust, glitter and eagerness to impress – just like Mummy and Daddy – Ava goes about being effortlessly brilliant, amazing everyone without fail but never caring one jot whether they were even vaguely interested – nothing like Mummy or Daddy at all. Frequently I'll say 'well done' and she'll look through me like I'm not even there. In fact, I think it's fair to say she reserves for me the sort of look that I am said to give so many of the guests I meet on my stage! Frightening . . .

It's like she can see right through the bullshit that all parents create to have the world make sense to young children. She will look at me like she's on to me and just exasperated by the fairytales that I thought all little girls believed in sometimes.

Not long before Christmas, she was making a bit of a noise in the middle of the night. I went in to check that she was OK. She was, but determined to be noisy enough to wake the others. I told her to pipe down, alas to no avail. I demanded that she be quiet, again I got nowhere. Panicking and fresh out of anything to negotiate with I looked down at my four-year-old and said, 'Look, Ava, if you don't behave, Daddy's going to have to phone Santa. Daddy will tell Santa that Ava's being naughty and if Santa hears that he might decide not to bring you any presents this year!' Being forty years my daughter's senior I assumed adult intelligence had won the day and felt quite pleased with myself for so creatively snuffing out Ava's little rebellion. I had struck a blow for grown-ups everywhere, this parenting lark was easy, right? Wrong!

No sooner had I smugly finished my little ultimatum than Ava was up and over to the phone. She lifted it off the receiver, casually sauntered back and dangled it in front of my face. With one of those trademark looks and the sort of contempt a teenager reserves for rebuking an embarrassing parent, she cut me down. 'Go on then,' was all she said. I swear if we were in a comic strip there would have been a bubble coming out of her head with the thought, 'Look, don't try and fool me with all this Santa rubbish. I don't believe it, and I'm only going along with it because I don't want to upset my older sister. I know what you're doing but frankly you're pathetic!'

It didn't end there. We went to see a Santa in a local grotto. Alice was typically excited, like every other child there. Again there was only one exception. While Alice gave Santa her wish list, sat on his knee, said thank you and struggled to contain herself, Ava just looked at him like he was a fraud. When Santa asked what was wrong, Ava said, 'you've changed.' Fair play, Little Miss Marple was spot on. That year's Santa was different to the one from the year before and Ava wasn't being duped by any festive nonsense for one second!

At other times, when the madness of playtime has erupted in shrieks all over our house, I will catch a glimpse of her. She'll be playing quietly, just observing the chaos. She's like a little Buddha, musing on how we conspire to make it all look so frenzied when the complexities of modern life are so easy to understand. I can almost hear her thinking, 'Look at you, you're all weird you are. This house is a madhouse. I don't know why I'm living here but I guess I'll have to go along with it until I'm old enough to get a place of my own.'

Don't get me wrong, Ava is not rude. She too is cute and sweet and impossibly beautiful. She just can't be bothered to put up with all the affected little rituals the rest of us build into each day to make us feel better about ourselves. Etiquette and pleasantries go out the window if she feels anything is a waste of her time and she reverts to being brilliantly dreadful . . .

Recently she got given an award at school for being a good girl, apparently the best in class. This was all well and good for Ava but she clearly couldn't see the need for any big hoo-hah in morning assembly. The headmistress made an announcement and welcomed Ava to collect her prize – part won for *politeness* no less – but my daughter just looked at the poor lady like she'd pissed on her shoes! Not a word, nothing. Unbelievable.

If you ask Ava if she'd like a biscuit, she doesn't bother taking one then perhaps going back for another if she's still peckish. No, without hesitation and in all seriousness she'll respond, 'Yes please, I'll have seven.' Seven! Many's the time I've wondered if she's being deliberately deadpan. Is she doing it for comic effect? Does she even know how funny she is? And where does she get this attitude from? Is she related to Jack Dee? Do I need to get him to do a DNA test?!

I've seen Ava strip half-naked without warning in a school nativity play. I've watched amazed as she wanders off to get away from it all and think to herself in the garden. While Alice will be wanting to play games all the time, indoors with us, Ava, more often than not, would prefer to put on her wellies and go for a little walk. On her own. She's four going on thirty-four!

When she does deign to come back inside, she joins in nonchalantly with whatever we're playing and generally wipes the floor with all of us. We recently bought a Nintendo Wii and everyone gathered round for a family bowling tournament. I feared tears as two young sisters went head-to-head with what I thought was a grown-ups' game they might struggle to get to grips with, but the only ones floundering were us oldies! Alice demolished Mummy, Daddy and a couple of their friends too but way out ahead was the one, the only, Ava. She was getting strike after strike, turkey after turkey (three strikes in a row) and she never once broke stride or sweat. It was amazing – she wasn't fussed but the rest of our jaws were on the floor!

With my other kids, I've got a pretty good idea of roughly what they might become, roughly where they might finish up and the origin of the talents they'll use to get them there. With Ava, though I just have no idea.

Henry might well end up, as his mother hopes, a charming, swashbuckling polo player, mixing happily with high society. I'll no doubt be doing my best to thrust a club in his hand and guide him towards the nearest golf course! Either way his personality and charm will endear him to most people he meets. I think he'll have plenty of girls swooning over him, and the confidence with which he is already waltzing through life will surely open a great many doors for him.

Alice, as I have said, will be a sweet, loving and effervescent star of whichever stage she chooses as her own. She'll delight, she'll dazzle and despite a few romantic hiccups along the way, I know she'll do well. She's her Daddy's Girl for now but her time will come.

And what of Ava? It would not surprise me if Mystic Meg looked me square in the eyes and proclaimed that my Ava-Pumpkin would grow up to be anything from revered world leader to a real-life wizard! Her brilliance is captivating, her individuality truly unique. I don't know where she gets so much of her fledgling greatness from, I just know that if she put her mind to it she could do anything ... in fact she regularly does.

17

Chivalry, Shrivelled

As someone who barely comes close, I know more than most that you really can't please all of the people all of the time. Nobody can and nothing ever has. The most popular leaders in history have always had their detractors, the funniest jokes ever written will always leave some people cold. For every majority that 'gets' it there will always be a minority who won't. Even the very best of humanity, those touched by divine inspiration, have been brought down by Man's jealousies and failure to understand. Jesus? Crucified. Gandhi? Shot dead. Even Simon Cowell can't convince the whole world of his greatness! Isn't it the best mankind can hope for that we agree on a few things that will make scurrying about on this planet that bit easier to bear for all of us? And NO exceptions. Yes, there will always be causes and campaigns that divide the human race but over the course of our history I would have thought that we'd have begun to agree on at least a few things by now – the need for common decency, for a start.

Things like tolerance and politeness are surely not beyond us. These should be treated as everyday realities we take for granted not aspirations we have to loudly campaign for. Now, I know it's hard. Humankind, especially where race and religion are concerned, has not exactly always been a beacon of tolerance over the years. And politeness? Well, I guess we are all capable of having a bad day. Stressed to the point of my eyeballs bursting in their sockets, I'm sure I've forgotten to say 'please' or 'thank you' once or twice. I make a point of always trying to be as courteous as I can but there will have been times when I've been too distracted or frustrated to be as polite as the person talking to me deserved. These temporary lapses are acceptable in anyone but what I really can't stand is the deliberate lack of common decency that so many take as their right to inflict on others!

I'm not talking about raised voices or tempers in a heated debate. I'm not even talking about a slip of the tongue or abuse handed out in the heat of the moment. These things will happen and might at least have some justification in context. What absolutely disgusts me though is the way in which some people in our society can throw an act of kindness back in another's face.

Not so long ago my father was the victim of just such an attack. He was not physically assaulted, his altercation involved a verbal exchange that lasted all of about five seconds but it left him as hollowed and humiliated as if he had been beaten up there and then. Travelling on the London Underground that day, my Old Man was mercilessly mugged of his dignity.

You may already have heard about or indeed read about my father in my first book, *I'm Only Being Honest*. I won't repeat the same details here. Suffice to say he is every inch the Old English gent of a bygone era. He's a man who spent thirty-four years working with the Royal Household and for whom his marriage and children are everything. He is the very bastion of the sorts of traditional family values this country would do well to embrace anew. He is charm personified, the epitome of good manners and the last word on the right and proper way of doing things. He's a bit of an old tart as well but that's another story and not the point I am making here!

Anyway, my father was travelling on a typically crowded Tube in the London rush hour. He was making his way from Paddington to Baker Street and whilst the carriage he was sat in wasn't exactly brimming it was filling steadily at each stop. As an elderly man of 75 he was grateful to have found a seat at the start of his journey. Jostling for position and coming up for clean air between draughts of the sweaty armpit your face has been forced into would never be my father's thing at all. Still, old or not and no matter the discomfort he might subject himself to by standing among the commuting sardines, he would always offer his seat to anyone he thought more deserving. It is a testament to his enduring values and sense of propriety that he would still think so many in this country more worthy of something so simple as a seat on a train than him.

One such example got on about midway through his journey. She was, he said, a nice enough looking lady but clearly a very heavily pregnant one who seemed to be struggling in her maternity dungarees. My dad told me she was shifting about uncomfortably. She was being squeezed and buffeted about the carriage as the train hiccupped out of the station and lurched along the line. Seeing a damsel he thought was in distress my father immediately offered his seat to the pregnant lady. What he got back made him wish he'd never bothered.

Here was a woman laden down with big bump, bigger bag, and getting bashed from pillar to post. My dad is the sort who will open doors for any female passing through, he'll hold the chair out for my mum before they sit down to dinner and bend down to pick up anything that might flutter out of a woman's purse, just to save them the bother (or in the hope that he might find a tenner on the floor!) Instinctively he offered the seat he would no doubt have been much happier to remain in, solely to spare this expectant mother the worst of the traumas of being trapped on a Tube. And her response to this kind offer?

'Do you know what's wrong with this f**king country? It's sexist old pigs like you who think that women like me can't stand up! Well I can and I don't want your f**king seat so sit back down yourself and keep it!'

My dad, a venerable old man of pride and standards was shocked to his core. He was humiliated in front of the whole carriage. He sat down, flushed pink with embarrassment and was left to reflect on what had just happened for the rest of his journey. Nobody else said a word, in fact a few just sniggered.

Now, Dad is the very stuff of stiff upper lips, of keeping one's emotions in check and not being given to unbecoming high spirits or hysteria. It was therefore all the more shocking to see him so visibly upset when he returned home from his ordeal. He was searching himself for answers as to what he did wrong. He was confused and could not fathom how the world he knew had seemingly changed so much, how attitudes could be transformed so completely, and right before his very eyes. My blood boils just to think of what he must have gone through that day, I know he would have been mortified as he slumped back in that seat and tried to make sense of what had just happened. Back at home, and days later when he had finally stopped brooding, the only conclusion he could come up with was a classic line I've never forgotten. 'It was the dungarees, I should have known,' was all he said and with that the matter was closed!

To make a man like my dad rethink all he has ever stood for is the very worst indictment I can think of to reproach this lady's actions. I could vent my spleen in condemnation, I could return fire and call her every name under the sun and she'd probably deserve it. I could become every bit the spitting demon my wife turned into at the height of her antenatal hormonal rages, but that would be to miss a much more important point. All of us can forgive emotional blips, the ups and downs of life and love – especially throughout a pregnancy – and anyone can have a bad day. But to humiliate a kind old man for doing nothing more than sacrifice his own seat to spare another human being some discomfort is just plain disgusting. How can anyone view those actions as sexist? I'm all for gender equality in every area of our lives but I don't think it has to be at the expense of good manners nor any kind of chivalrous behaviour. Just like my dad, I'd always offer my seat to someone I thought needed it more, to do the right thing and behave like a true gentleman. Equal rights don't come into it, doing what's right does.

Unbelievably, now, in this country of ours, we have signs on buses instructing passengers to act with the gallantry that should be as instinctive to all of us as it is to my father. 'Please give up this seat for elderly passengers', we are told.

Jeez, how low have we sunk that we actually need signposts telling us to help our senior citizens? What next, signs telling us not to kick young babies in the face? Offering a seat to a lady, helping the frail, looking out for those less fortunate – that stuff should come naturally to all of us.

How sad it is that my dad gets barracked for doing the sort of good turn that has always come as second nature to him. How sad too that our society now deems it necessary to signpost the decent way to behave because too few know how. Saddest of all for me though was the fact that as my dad came to terms with his verbal assault that day, he truly considered whether in future he should just shut up, keep his head down and not interact at all with anyone else on public transport. He didn't want to risk further confrontation and thought that staying silent might now be the only way to spare himself further humiliation.

What a tragedy that the country has come to this, that we're all getting to a point where thinking of oneself and looking aggressively after Number One is the only way to get by.

18

Who's Up for Feeling Sexy?

Let me ask you a question: would you, yes you sitting there and reading this right now, would *you* like to be considered hot? You know, sexy, good looking, *Hot*?

I most definitely would. I'd certainly take that over most of the alternatives the other end of the spectrum has to offer. I'm not saying I am desperate to be seen as sexy, mind. To be honest, at forty-four years of age I am not that bothered anymore. I am pretty much beyond caring about what remains of my sex appeal, if indeed there is anything left at all. Baldness? Yes. Cleanliness? Absolutely. Life as a potential sex god? Hmmm, no. Final answer. That said, I know I'm not alone in thinking that to be seen as hot stuff has got to be better than being written off as some butt-faced oaf with a face that could curdle custard!

The reason I ask the initial question is simple. One of my very good friends went out on a date recently, with a lady who was soon to become her lesbian lover. All was going well, or so my friend thought, until she let slip that she thought her date looked 'hot'. Not sweating like a pig over a bonfire with make-up running all down her face but hot, hot. The wine had taken hold and her tongue had loosened sufficiently to start speaking the language of love . . . Well, lust at least. It was clear theirs was a mutual attraction founded over many weeks of online chatting about hobbies and shared interests. So, seeing that her date, who she'd admired for so many reasons beyond good looks was also very attractive, my friend leaned over and gave what she thought and hoped would be a well-received compliment. She could not have been more wrong!

In fairness, it's always a bit of a gamble to go with the 'you're so sexy', 'God I fancy you', or 'oooh, you're smoking hot' so soon into a date. Retain the mystique, keep a little bit back, play it a bit Pokerface – don't go 'all in' the first chance you get. (Prematurity is a problem that can plague many aspects of a relationship!)

These days, many of my guests tell me, the preferred arena for those sorts of risqué declarations is the internet, or even the text message. If that's the case at least try and email or text whilst sober, 'cos how many people have woken up in the morning, after one too many the night before, only to have their hangover made ten times worse by a quick flick through their sent items? It might be tough for nervous first-nighters to avoid alcohol at dinner – anything to calm the nerves, right? – but beware the honesty it may unleash once the beers have really started flowing.

Initially I guess, it's best to spend that talk-time just getting to know each other. With each glass of wine poured the person sat opposite may well be growing increasingly beautiful while the thoughts in your head grow ever more sinful. Even so, be careful not to declare too much too soon. Like the person who says 'I love you' to a partner only just used to the idea of dating, reciprocation is never guaranteed. Going in feet first with a fistful of poetry will undoubtedly freak a fair few out so it's best to choose certain words carefully, reveal certain feelings gradually.

My friend knew all this and she assures me that wine was not a factor in what happened next. All she did, she was at pains to point out, was look at her date and tell her she looked hot! She maintains she did it discretely, politely and at the appropriate juncture. She was not wolf-whistling a stranger or leering lustfully at someone she'd no knowledge of. This date was the culmination of weeks of playful chat.

Now there's not a great deal wrong in that is there, saying someone looks hot in that context? It might be a bit of a 'come-on', it is certainly a bit cheeky and I can just about see how some might think it too forward. People of my parents' generation might have preferred a 'you look delightful tonight', perhaps a 'beautiful' or even a 'delectable'. Going with 'hot' may well be a bit blunt but such boldness of expression is forgivable at least for being in keeping with the times and I can't really see why it would have caused my friend's date, a single woman in her thirties, the slightest bit of offence. In fact, if out on a first date with the woman who's been try woo you online for weeks, there's not many better signals to give out is there?

Well, I'm sorry to disappoint but the lady she'd conversed with quite openly and probably quite naughtily online, a woman she found genuinely attractive and who'd enjoyed all of their intimate flirtations to this point, apparently recoiled in horror. Leaving my friend dazed and confused, not to mention the whole of the restaurant silent, she thundered, 'DON'T YOU OBJECTIFY ME!' Woah! Where did that come from?

It no doubt took an age for the silence in the room to be replaced by an awkward scraping of cutlery on crockery as stunned diners slowly returned their focus to the meals before them. My friend was dumbstruck. She did not know what she had done. You'd think she'd just farted in her date's face by the look being shot back at her. Her date was genuinely livid. Clearly this lady was in tune with feminist doctrine, and did not feel at ease with the disempowering connotations of the girl she fancied regarding her as 'hot'. She, I presume, did not want anyone's eyes to see her *only* as object, no matter how sexy. She said she found it demeaning or degrading in some way. Fair enough I guess, if that's how she really felt, but I can't quite see it myself. I don't understand why this lady would respond in this way, given all they'd previously discussed and everything they declared they liked in one another.

I mean, there's a world of difference between being told you're hot and being expected to parade around in your panties looking hot for all to see, like it is the only thing you're good for. It is only one of a million layers to a person, granted, but it's one that most of us would want working for and not against us, surely. In my friend's date's case what would the alternative be? What indeed would have been the best way for my mate to give an *honest* compliment in that situation, one that was truthfully representative without causing offence? 'I'm sorry but I have to tell you, your emails are thought-provoking, your choice of wine simply divine and the books you've read just rock my world. So please, darling, crack on with dessert so we can get back home and text each other about Chaucer!' Even my most prudish, reserved or most staunchly feminist mates all like to be told

144

they look nice when they dress up to go out, and saying they do indeed look nice has nothing to do with me objectifying anyone, even the ones who genuinely do look sexy!

Take my wife. She can be by turns beautiful, sexy and sometimes so bloody hot I just want to tear her clothes off. There's a time and a place of course but she can still make my pulse race in a way that provokes thoughts that some may consider every bit as objectionable as they sometimes are objectifying! And she's OK with that, most people are. Sex is important in any relationship, feeling sexy is important for any person's esteem and knowing your partner thinks you're sexy, amongst *all* the other things of course, can't be anything but important too, surely?

If some people can really mistake such a glowing modern day endorsement of one part of themselves, they really need to get a life. The date would not have been suggested in the first place if there wasn't an intellectual respect there, a mutual appreciation of the views, values and intelligence of both of them, would there? I just haven't got time for all those people who twist nice words given in good faith into something that keeps them the victim of a supposed oppression, which doesn't truly exist for them. It has the same effect on me as people who play the race card unfairly or claim sexism without foundation. Not only is it unfair on one person trying to do the right thing, however clumsily, it is also offensive to the genuine victims who are struggling against the reality of oppression, each and every day.

Unsurprisingly, my friend's liaisons with She-Who-Must-Not-Be-Objectified did not last long. She did rescue the dinner though and did enough to end up making coffee for two back at her place that very night. Thereafter she reported

that her new friend was only too happy to be objectified –
passionately, noisily, and all night long!

Good luck to her but it wouldn't have washed with me.
If someone was that bothered by a genuine compliment I'd
harmlessly given I reckon any desire I had for objectifica-
tion would shrivel on the spot. In fact the only thing I'd be
objectifying from that moment on would be the number of
a taxi to get me the hell out of there!

19

In Deep at the Shallow End?

It is often said that celebrities are quite a shallow, insincere bunch. And it is easy to see why. Drift into any party where a smattering of famous faces are dotted and you might see them ditch the friends they came with in order to make a beeline for each other. The unknowns get dropped, like high-carb canapés at the buffet, the minute any 'well known' walks through the door, or so the legend goes. I've been accused of the same, of turning my back on 'us' to cravenly pursue acceptance as one of 'them'. I've been tut-tutted for daring to leave the team I came with and introduce myself to other presenters, sometimes even – shock, horror! – ones from rival tribes! I've been sneered at and told that sneaking off to chat with another so-called celebrity was sure proof that I'd changed, become just like all the rest and therefore must think I'm better than everyone else. The charge laid at my door was basically one of élitism, a snobbery that sees only fellow celebs as worthy of my time and company. What a load of old rubbish!

Whilst it's uncanny how celebrities always *do* seem to huddle together at functions, I have to tell you that there is nothing sinister going on. I have made a few famous friends through work but none of us see ourselves as better than anyone else. I know I am not élitist and am perfectly happy in most people's company – fame never comes into it. Equally, though, I don't see what is wrong with popping over to say 'hi' to someone at a party!

To be honest, the novelty of being invited to the odd star-studded event has still not worn off on me yet. I still pinch myself whenever I'm asked to attend one of those glittering ceremonies I only ever used to read about in the papers. At heart I am still the little boy from Coley Park, Reading who can't quite believe his luck or that all this is really happening to him. It's a bit like the first time I turned up to film my show in Manchester. Just round the corner was the Corrie set. Now, I've been a fan of *Coronation Street* for thirty-odd years and in fact I still am. I was like an excited kid in a sweet shop when I was first told I could walk the famous cobbles and have a nose around The Rovers! And imagine what it was like when I first saw Ken Barlow queuing up for chips with me in the canteen!

Football's another passion, and my team is West Ham, so picture the scene recently at a Football Writers' dinner, when the god that is Harry Redknapp came over and stopped to have a chat with *me*! At that moment, five years of telly experience went out the window and I was completely lost for words. It gets worse; weeks before that encounter I was just having a quiet dinner in a local restaurant when Chris Evans breezed by. Again I was struck dumb. I wanted to say something but couldn't. I wanted to wish him well for his new Radio 2 *Breakfast Show* but was welded in silence to my seat. Eventually, I did it; I got up and went over. Many would not, lots don't but I am one of those who can't help myself.

If I see someone I might never get the chance to meet again, and especially someone I admire, I'll go over. *Carpe diem* and all that. 'Seize the day, grasp the nettle, go over and risk making a fool of yourself if you have to, Jez, but at least you can say that, yes, you actually talked *to* someone you'd previously only talked about.' Alas, my stuttering away clumsily to Mr Evans probably didn't make the best impression but I'm glad I made the effort all the same. It was no skin off his nose and no one I returned to at our table felt bereft because of an absence that tore me away for all of about 180 seconds!

Now, I'm not stupid and I know there is a lot of fakery from people who work in the entertainment industry. The average celebrity awards ceremony is not necessarily the best advert for the sincerity of human emotion. No one can deny the simpering superficiality on show in some quarters or indeed the sickening displays of sycophancy on display in others. There are jealousies and rivalries and petty positioning going on all around but not by everyone and not in a way that is so different to most other works parties I've seen in my life. People hang on the arm of the boss, laugh at his/her bad jokes or flirt ridiculously to get ahead at office shin-digs up and down the land. It is no different at a typical glitzy red carpet bash – they, essentially, are just glorified office parties for a load of people who all work in the same industry. Bad behaviour goes on, people have too much to drink and show themselves up just like they do anywhere else. People can be fake and insincere for myriad motivations but no more so in this line of work than any other. The main difference for me now is that paparazzi are on hand to capture my every potential disgrace whereas before I might have had to go it alone with the office photocopier!

TV jobs can bring their stars a wonderful life and status that would be difficult to leave behind but even tougher to have taken away. So, however tactless and crass some approaches, I can understand that desire to get proactive about job-hunting in a room full of potential employers. Lots of times certain celebs would have done well to steer clear of the free booze before making their play but they've been no worse than the lawyer who glad-hands his boss to try and make partner, or the producer who drones drunkenly on to a commissioner about why he's so deserving of promotion.

Given the ease with which celebrities are supposed to make friends, another thing I find quite bizarre is the frequency with which I am forced to defend the friendships I have made with people who just happen to be well known. I'm often asked to justify how it is that two famous people can possibly like each other! Does this not seem a bit strange to anyone else? We all pick up different friends from different stages and times in our lives – school, university, the areas we've lived, the places we've worked etc., etc. In no other walk of life though has anyone been so suspicious of the friends I've made and kept. When I stacked bananas at Marks & Spencer nobody would have batted an eyelid if I said I was going out for a few beers with a mate I'd met who worked the tills. Get a little famous and make a famous friend though, and the knives come out. Then the questions. And then the judgements.

One of my best friends from my last fifteen years in radio and television is none other than Noddy Holder. Yes, he of Slade fame and the one who screams 'It's Chriiiiiiiiiiistmas!'

into our ears about fifty times a day each festive season. Now, I've known him for many years, we've done a lot of work together and I couldn't find a bad word to say against him if I tried. He's intelligent, loyal, trustworthy – an all-round good, true, salt of the earth bloke. However, when I get asked which celebrities out there I would honestly consider a friend and Noddy's name crops up, people scoff. It's like he's not cool enough or big enough for them, like he's not sufficiently up the *Heat* hierarchy to accord me any credibility. It's the same with my dear, dear friend Derek Thompson, face of Channel 4 racing and the hardest-working man I know in this business. What's that all about? I'm not friends with someone because of the column inches they command. I'd be no more proud to call David Beckham a mate than Derek Thompson – their global pulling power just doesn't come into it.

A friend is a friend is a friend – for the same reasons in my life as anyone else's. There's no agenda. Some people I click with, some I don't. Some people I am proud to have in my life, others I'm happy to avoid at all costs – that's just normal isn't it? I'm sure plenty of people would give me a wide berth. Worse, I imagine there's a fair few more who must recoil every time they're forced to admit that I am in fact one of their friends – I must be the most denied celebrity mate on the planet!

I don't have loads of celebrity friends. I don't go around trying to collect them either. I happen to know a lot of good people who also happen to be celebrities, and a fair few have, over time, gone on to become good friends, but that process has been no different from getting to know any other buddy through all my jobs in the past.

It's like some people want to check my mobile and count up the famous numbers it contains just so they can tell how far down the Celebrity 'It' League I am as a result! I find the level of interest a bit baffling, but since people do seem to want to know, I might as well explain. Of all the people I've met over the past five years it is Eamonn Holmes who has made the most lasting impression on me. He offered great advice from the start but has backed it up every day since with the time, affection, loyalty and kindness that marks all good friends out from run-of-the-mill, everyday mates. He helped talk me through those first scrapes with the press that terrify all newcomers to the industry. He gave me some useful pointers when writing my first book, has looked after me whenever we have worked together and has always been there. Most recently he has given me the confidence to be who I am, to be more proud of all I do and to basically be more comfortable in my own skin. His is always the most stellar advice. When I was starting out he urged me to focus on the proper priorities, cut through the crap and told me in no uncertain terms that all any of us should concentrate on whilst working in this industry is 'paying off the mortgage and educating the kids'. Of course he's dead right.

Chris Tarrant said something similar to me when I was working at Capital Radio. I used to see him looking absolutely knackered whenever I passed him in the corridor and it was clear that with his *Breakfast Show*, numerous TV projects and an Italian clothing company to manage, he was burning both ends of any candle he could get his hands on. He wasn't interested in slowing down either.

He explained that everyone should say 'yes' to the projects they can, while they can. He knew the offers would dry up one day and he wanted to make the most of his privileged position before his star faded and the phone calls started filtering elsewhere. I get that and have resolved to work as hard as I can on whatever I can before someone tells me my time is up. Hopefully the final bit of advice from Eamonn will ring true for us all. He once told me that longevity in our careers is all any of us should be seeking, and achieving it, he said, is as much about the offers we turn down as the ones we accept. Eamonn's right, he always seems to be.

Good friends aside, Mr Holmes is not the only celebrity I've spoken to whose advice has been invaluable. My very first meeting with some of the various movers and shakers in the industry came at a party hosted by ITV. Nervous like it was my first day at 'big school', I was being shown around and introduced to all my stablemates on the channel. I felt a bit like the wet-behind-the-ears stockbroker being ushered around the grand old bank that had stood proudly for a hundred years. I did not know what to expect but was on guard as old hands viewed the new upstart with suspicion. I recognised plenty of faces but knew absolutely none of the people. I felt a little out of my depth but then a Loose Woman strode into my life and spoke to me in a way I've never forgotten!

Carol McGiffin could see me worrying. She could probably also hear me thinking, 'Am I ever going to fit in around here, what have I got myself into?' when she came over and cut in with an, 'All right mate?' which thankfully put me right at ease. Referring to the famous faces, she said, 'Look, I love it and it's great but let me just warn you about two things. Number One, they'll air kiss your face and then slag you off behind your back. Number Two, they'll take your mobile number and never call!' Do you know what? She was spot on.

Meeting Carol as soon as I did was brilliant for me. Our brief encounter showed me the way and gave me all I needed by way of a template for how I wanted to be myself. From that moment I vowed I'd always take people in this business at face value and treat them as they treated me, just like her, no matter what I'd heard or read about them before. That philosophy has so far served me well.

Anyway, if meeting the people with whom I might one day be working was scary, my first crack at the work itself was truly terrifying.

As soon as I'd signed the deal to front *The Jeremy Kyle Show* I was instructed to get up to speed with life in front of the cameras. I thought I was going to be broken in gently on other shows – five minutes here, five minutes there – whilst my own show's production team got everything together for our launch in the meantime. That made sense to me. What actually happened was crazy . . .

My first bit of experience as host of a TV show was not as a bit-part presenter of some small throwaway filler item on a barely-watched show. No, I was to be the bloody co-host of *This Morning*! Now, after five years hosting *The Jeremy Kyle Show* I feel pretty confident as a presenter. It is what I do. I am well used to the cameras, autocue, audiences and all the rest of the stuff that goes round the main bit of actually talking to our guests and trying to point them in the right direction. Things may look fairly slickly edited on my own show but people tend to forget that our episodes are pre-recorded. The cock-ups I still make five years down the line can be snipped out, links I read wrongly can be re-recorded – and frequently are.

This Morning is a different beast altogether. That is a two-hour marathon of *live* television – not the ideal place for a rookie to earn his stripes with some time in the broadcasting trenches. On my show I only ever have a maximum of two people talking to me through the flesh-coloured prawn that is my earpiece. The director, who tells me where to stand and which cameras to look at for the bits I have to read, and the editor, who keeps us pointing in the right direction where codes of conduct and content are concerned. On *This Morning*, Phil and Holly have earpieces through which anyone in an overcrowded gallery can and does speak! Directors, producers, graphics assistants, vision mixers and a million other people whose jobs I don't understand all twitter away in the background whilst the presenter stares down the camera and talks to the viewer like they are the only one watching.

I admit I was completely flummoxed within about ten seconds. It was how I imagined going mad to be. There were about sixteen voices in my head at any one time – and none of them were mine! People were talking to me and to each other in one big indecipherable din. I didn't know where to look or what to do. My mind's own voice couldn't get a word in, it was drowned out by everyone else's. Anyone watching would have seen my head fall to one side, gormless, blank and confused, like a dog that can't make sense of its owner's whistle. My jaw fell open but nothing came out. I desperately wanted to spout some drivel but all I could manage was a trickle of dribble. All around people were waiting for me to say something, anything. Thankfully I had another saviour that day: the wonderful Lorraine Kelly. She helped me through, held my hand and papered over the cracks like the true pro she is. I'll forever be grateful for her help that day, and her politeness and courteousness every time since.

After guiding me through the first show Lorraine made way for another co-host on my second day's filming. Shaking like a shitting dog and petrified that Lorraine had scarpered because she couldn't bear to carry me through another doomed broadcast, my next chaperone was to be the one and only Fern Britton.

Her introduction set the tone and showed in ten seconds the kindness of spirit and down-to-earth deftness of touch that makes her so universally loved – by all those she works with every bit as much as everyone watching at home (quite the achievement by the way – you'd be surprised how many presenters can just about manage one out of those two!) As I trembled, there was a loud knock at my dressing room door. A familiar and friendly squawk came from outside. 'Kindly move back from the door, very large lady with a cup of tea coming through!' I was won over instantly and looked after thoroughly thereafter by one of the best in the business.

It's probably fair to say that I didn't impress too many people in those first couple of days presenting *This Morning*. I hadn't mastered the art of reading aloud nor could I deal with all of those other little technical hurdles that move a show from A to B. However, in between the bumbling, the sweating and the shaking I did manage to find my own voice among the squatters who gatecrashed my brain whenever I put my earpiece back in. No one saw fit to release the hounds each time I made a mistake. We all persisted. And I was grateful for one proper chance to be myself, and stand up for a new friend.

That first fateful day with Lorraine Kelly on *This Morning* saw us interviewing Robert Downey Jr. At the time he was making some sort of comeback. If memory serves he was fresh out of his latest rehab programme and on to proclaim a clean bill of health and boast a new, even cleaner lifestyle. He also may have wanted to talk about getting into the music business, I'm not sure. Whatever, I know he definitely did want to talk about being off drugs and being a nice guy, so I settled back and followed Lorraine's lead for the interview. She introduced herself courteously but all Downey Jr could muster by way of reply was, 'Nice tits!' I forgot completely that I was on TV, and probably that it is not the done thing for mouthy upstarts to be offending Hollywood A-listers on their first morning on the job. As ever, I couldn't help myself.

'Oi you!' I said. 'I thought you were here to build a new start after all that drug stuff, and to talk about your music – you can leave her alone!'

A new TV motormouth may well have been born at that moment without me even realising it! To be honest though, I was just glad that Robert Downey Jr didn't react in a way that would probably have had me fired on the spot. He could have shouted, screamed or thrown a tantrum. He could have killed the interview right there and stropped back to his dressing room but to his credit he took my medicine like a man and didn't answer back. He was fine with both of us after that, and the perfect gentleman throughout the rest of the interview. Phew!

By the end of that week I had just about shown enough for ITV to persist with me. We launched *The Jeremy Kyle*

Show a little later on that summer, in 2005, and thankfully things went well. The sort of life I once led gradually morphed into the one I now lead – thankfully without too many changes and, happily, with a few more friends.

Like Carol McGiffin I 'love it' too, this industry *is* great and the life it gives me is wonderful. Like anything, it is not without its problem people and potential pitfalls but, just as Eamonn surmised, I too want it to last as long as possible and will always work as hard as I can to make sure that happens. Carla and I will travel the world the minute it all comes to an end when, as Chris Tarrant warned, the offers stop coming in. Until then it is head down, work hard and do all I can to pay off the mortgage, put the kids through school and save a little something for my dotage.

To those who ask and a few who've accused I, truly would never deny that, yes, this job has changed my life. Yes, I've met some famous people. Yes, I've been to some swanky parties and got a few celeb friends whose numbers help fill up my phone. But, at my core and pretty much overall, actually very little has changed at all. I am still the person I always was and my outlook is still the same. The first plank of my every ambition is always, educate the kids, put a roof over our heads and ensure we have food on the table. Given that my youngest child is nine months old, it will be a long time yet before that begins to change.

20

I'm A Slobrity – Get Me Out of Here
(and into a gym)!

I have been asked to comment on this country's collective expanding waistline on numerous occasions. It is an issue that has grown quite close to my own slowly clogging heart, not least because I have three young children and am approaching an age at which obesity becomes a big risk. I've visited a hospital in New York that caters for hugely overweight Americans – extreme examples of morbid obesity whose 'addiction' to food I couldn't class as anything but a life-threatening disease, despite having arrived as something of a sceptic. On the other hand, I've met a fair few closer to home whose battle with the bulge could be easily won with just a few tweaks to their lifestyle and a big change in diet.

When I was approached by the *Sun* to write a brief column on the subject I did so on the back of some alarming figures that had just been released. Unbelievably, we were told that UK kids spend up to ten hours per day staring at screens. Apparently only second to American children, our 7–16-year-olds spend an average of *four months* each year gawping at televisions, computer games, the mobiles or the web! Even more frightening was the revelation that children deprived of their electronic entertainment fixes were now starting to exhibit signs of depression – some reported they felt 'lost' without them. Some kids were hooked and many more were ballooning in weight as they beached themselves permanently in front of their favoured box.

I admit I probably turned into Grumpy Fifties Dad there and then. I ranted and raved in disbelief, turning my fire on the lethargy that is allowed to grip so many so young. And I think I'm still entitled to that rage. In part. I mean, is it so wrong to hark back to times gone by when all kids ran themselves ragged after school, playing football in the park or chasing each other round the streets? I accept that some parents nowadays may be reluctant to let their children go wandering off alone. I know many who are genuinely scared to let their kids out of their sight for just one second. But has people's paranoia about a potential abduction been whipped up to a point where parents are now content to have their kids inside all the time, wasting a *third* of their lives vegetating in front of a screen? If the figures I've read are to be believed, the threat from paedophiles has not changed much over the past twenty or thirty years. However, the threat posed to the health of this nation's children by changing lifestyles and diet definitely has. I'm not advocating the abandoning of all reason and I'd never suggest that any parent send their son or daughter off anywhere inappropriate without adequate supervision. Equally though I think some parents could do much more to take a lead in liberating their sofas from the children whose overweight arses have become permanently anchored to them. Not enough are doing enough and it's time they stepped up to the mark.

I don't mean to be glib and I am certainly mindful of the tragic abductions we have all read about in recent years. But despite some horrific stories that have rightly received a lot of coverage in the media, it surely can't be the case that some crazed child-catcher lurks behind every corner. I do wonder if the fears of some parents are truly commensurate with the real level of threat out there. I mean, are they? Obviously, every parent's first instinct is to protect their child from potential harm, but locking them in the house and chaining them to a TV can't be the best way, not if their health is being so patently damaged as a result.

Let's face it, leaving the kids on the couch is hardly a passport to untold riches and opportunity! And it certainly won't guarantee their health and vitality either. We've all got to look out for our kids, of course, but that involves more than just protecting them from the dirty old man we fear might snatch them down the local park. To truly take care of our kids it is just as important to educate them about the choices underpinning a healthier lifestyle. There are just too many distractions available to them that involve no more physical exertion than I use on the toilet each morning, and some which require even less!

For as long as children need their parents to provide something to do when they're bored, those parents have a duty to enable their kids to get out of the house and to be as active as possible inside it. What's the alternative? To inflict a lazy life of obesity on your children merely because you could not be bothered to make a stand yourself is just crazy, criminal even, if social services keep on removing obese children from their parents they feel are abusing them with food!

Get out there with them. Go to the park and kick a ball about. Make the time wherever possible – that was my sole policy on the subject until very recently. I wasn't convinced by the arguments of people who insisted not all computer games were bad. I thought they were just mindless rubbish packaged in clever marketing. I couldn't see myself as being anything other than dead against them. That was until I bought one for myself!

OK, OK, I didn't buy it for myself exactly, I went the way of so many dads at Christmas and allowed myself to be bullied into buying a Nintendo Wii for my children, presented on behalf of Santa of course. I squared it with myself thus: I did not believe for one second that my children were likely to become bloated couch potatoes overnight. They are far too active for that to happen. In fact, I figured that there would be times when I'd actually be praying that they would take time out to sit quietly for half an hour in front of a game when Carla and I were too exhausted to run around the house with them one more time. They are so full of beans – energetic and noisy and beautifully so – morning, noon and night that I couldn't see a problem with introducing a bit of computerised bowling and tennis to their lives. I've always maintained that a balance in their lifestyle is crucial. They hare around the house all day, I go swimming with them at the weekends, and we're forever messing about in the garden with them too. They are all on the go all the time and have lives that more than compensate for the odd biscuit they might munch (or indeed the odd seven my Ava might try and get her paws on!) An hour or two a week on a Wii, I concluded, would not do them too much harm – it wasn't like the only thing they were exercising was their thumb as they drooled goggle-eyed at the screen. There was no chance I would let that happen. Still, this Grumpy Old Man, who remembers playing sports the more traditional way, with a knackered cricket set in the Reading garden I always pretended was Lord's, viewed the new toy with suspicion!

Now, I'm not perfect. I'll admit I'm as guilty as the next parent of sometimes being too tired to want to play chase or do face-painting at all hours. I've been there on a Sunday morning, woken too early from a night that finished too late but instructed by bored children who could not care less to nevertheless get out of bed and entertain them. I confess, I have in the past reached for the Peppa Pig DVD and watched it with them the only way I know how when my head is banging and the rest of me is still screaming for sleep: eyes half-closed, daughter under each arm, laughing on command whenever nudged in the ribs and feigning excitement about the next bit of a programme we've all watched together a thousand times over! I'm not blind to the benefits of a TV when babysitting during a down day, but even so I had always mistrusted the pernicious influence computer games might have on my brood. Happily though, I stand corrected. That Nintendo Wii was one of the best presents 'Santa' ever brought down our chimney!

I'm no expert on the effects that an unsavoury gaming release might have on a child's development but what I have seen with my own eyes is how positive an influence a strictly monitored diet of computer gaming can have not just on my kids, but the whole family. Ever since that Wii was unwrapped we've regularly come together for on-screen tournaments that have helped keep us active as individuals and bonded as a family. We talk between rounds of the games we play. We're up, down and bouncing around together constantly and, little by little, getting a touch fitter whilst also feeling a bit closer. I never thought I'd be so into an area of life I thought irrelevant to me but I have to say I'm a fan. And a couple of hours of playing tennis on the Wii with Alice and Ava has the added bonus of knocking them out for the count when bedtime rolls around – brilliant.

My mind became more made up when I read recently of weight-loss mum, Lara Roberts. She apparently lost eight stone in a little less than two years by following a fitness regime worked out for her on her Nintendo Wii Fit. She obviously combined this with the right choices in other areas of her life but fair play to her and to anyone else who might be similarly inclined to give it a go – it has got to be better than having no go at all.

For my part, I am now a believer in the positive potential of some (not all) computer games. Aside from helping physical fitness and bonding us as a family I can see that being technically proficient in this arena can only aid the kids' development in, say, computer literacy. Getting au fait with the sorts of modern tools and technologies which will increasingly come to govern all our lives is probably sensible, and the earlier the better. It is certainly preferable to being left like me, the old man at the back of the class having constantly to ask everyone around him how to power his laptop or print a damn email! My kids now have a few games that brilliantly test their co-ordination and capacity to problem solve, too. They can brain train and play to their heart's content whilst I struggle alone in fury with something as simple as setting a password.

I have always been vehemently opposed to the disgraceful selling off of our schools' playing fields. That should never have been allowed to happen under any government. It has limited children's options to get out and be active, and partly as a response, schools have made what I initially thought was a faintly preposterous proposal to conduct PE lessons in part by using things like the Nintendo Wii Fit. I still disagree with those sell-offs and would resist any further attempts to pillage the playing fields I think all kids have a right to enjoy. Similarly I would always advocate having a proper game of tennis or cricket over their computerised namesakes. That said, I do have to concede we are where we are and we all have to make the best of what is available to us. Wishing those playing fields back is futile so we might as well embrace all we're left with whilst also exploiting new technology to help our kids get fitter. And if just one child is encouraged to get 'Wii fit' where slogging up and down a sports hall, embarrassed in front of his classmates, failed previously, that has to be a good thing. As I say, I don't think it is *the* solution but it can certainly be used to solve part of the problem that affects today's generation of children more than any previous one.

It is reckoned that ninety-five per cent of ten-year-olds in 1998 would wipe the floor with their counterparts of today in running tests. One in four boys starting school today are overweight and so are one in five girls! Surveys suggest that since 2002 there has been a fifty per cent drop in traditional childhood accidents usually spawned by tree climbing etc. However, in that same time the number of children suffering from, wait for it, *repetitive strain injury* has soared! Apparently our culture, that sees too many youngsters cooped up indoors and fed a diet of takeaways and TV, has left some with overworked thumbs, stressed to the point of exhaustion and laying limp, pale and listless on the sofa. This just won't do.

I won't shy away from my recent conversion and newly held conviction. I do honestly now believe that a computer console like the Nintendo Wii can bring some good to the health of everyone in my family, and not least the family unit itself. However such things need to be enjoyed in moderation and balanced against the need for proper exercise elsewhere – they should never come at the expense of outdoor pursuits. No computer game, no matter how much fun to play or energetic to get through can ever replace the cut and thrust of being involved in proper sports. Playing outside with a real bat and ball will always trump anything a computer might synthesise to replicate that sensation. It has to – the fresh air alone makes the garden or the park a better option than the front room. That has always been the case, it always will be and that's why it is imperative that parents seize the initiative to set the right example.

I am no poster boy for healthy living. The odd crafty fag here and there does me no favours at all but at least I eat fairly well, even though I know I could do better. I was once a chubby child but I don't feel sufficiently bovine to now join the ranks of 12 million dieters currently starving themselves towards a thinner figure in Britain. I am though about to right a terrible wrong by belatedly updating my gym membership! Yes, henceforth I am resolved, for the sake of a wife and children who have no need to see me wheezing as I flail about the garden with them, to embark on a new regime which should see me going to the gym about three times a week. I am no great fan of such places but I can also no longer ignore their worth. If I don't take action soon I stand on the verge of becoming the worst of all worlds – a fat skeleton! What little meat I do have on my bones has started to sag in all the wrong places whilst some of the bones could do with a bit more meat to start with! I think it's safe to assume I'll never be Mr Universe but I will try to plump up my twiglet limbs a touch and just try to become a little firmer and fitter all round. I'm not sure it'll help my dismal performance whenever I am trounced on the Wii by my two youngest daughters but it will at least represent a step in the right direction, for their sakes as much as my own.

All things being equal, my shift in attitude towards the gym might just turn out to be every bit as beneficial as the one I've just undergone in respect of things like the Wii itself.

21

Everyday Miracles

If we were still living in the Dark Ages, what I'm about to write would be taken as evidence of my descent into the evils of witchcraft. I'd likely be lynched and told my unspeakable words were the work of Satan. The high priests of the time would not believe me; instead they'd rush to tell the world I was in league with the devil. In fact, overall, that's not too different to how some speak about me now!

In all seriousness though, I wanted to take stock of just a few of those things that are now ten-a-penny but not too long ago were unfathomable concepts only the supernatural could explain.

We've been scurrying about on this planet for thousands of years and it is clear we've come a long way. These days though, the pace of change in our lives is so quick that I don't think any of us stop for long enough to properly take it all in. The everyday technological feats of the twenty-first century that astound me would until very recently have been regarded as the stuff of miracle. If I were writing this a few hundred years ago, I would have had to attribute all my speculations to the work of the Almighty himself, if I was to escape being torched at the local village bonfire! Back then mankind really couldn't make it up, all design was inherently, exclusively divine and the things we take for granted now could barely be imagined. Today we are used to the power of science and the capacity of the engineering it spawns to make so many of Man's dreams a reality. We all now expect these great advances and treat the arrival of the next big idea to make our lives a little easier with barely more than an indifferent shrug.

I'm often accused of being stuck in the Dark Ages (thanks!) so perhaps it is fitting that I still struggle to take in all we are now capable of. I'm not talking about the really huge projects that rightly stopped us all in our tracks. Space programmes, putting Man on the Moon and the many amazing examples of industrial engineering are all jaw-droppingly awe-inspiring and impossible for me to ever get my head round. But even more impressive to me, strangely, are the seemingly minor breakthroughs we have made that now benefit so many.

Take laser eye surgery. I know, I know – it's been around for years, everyone's had it done, boring, boring. Frankly though, I find it utterly amazing. It's essentially a cure for blindness! Where once I might have been reliant on a bona fide biblical miracle, now I can go to the local opticians and get both eyes fixed for four hundred quid! Not cheap I know, but then again not a whole hill of beans when weighed against the gift of renewed and recovered sight!

Graham, the psychotherapist from my show, had laser surgery on his eyes and so did Will, our floor manager. Both were apprehensive beforehand, who wouldn't be? I certainly don't fancy my chances of sitting still and staring calmly ahead as some Dr Evil in a white coat fixes my head into a clamp and starts burning strips into my eyeball with his 'la-zerrr'. No thank you. Another friend had the same proce-dure and she said that while there was no pain, she could actually *smell* her eye cooking as the surgeon sizzled away at it with his precision guided barbecue!

Nevertheless, afterwards all of them were evangelical about the brilliance of the modern day miracle they had just expe-rienced. After a few days of confinement, spent with Biggles goggles tied round their heads in a darkened room, they came blinking back out into the light and a new life where they could finally see clearly. In some cases for the very first time in their lives!

After the operation, Graham told me that waking up was no longer a blur but glorious pinpoint technicolour. There was no confused fumbling around for glasses he couldn't find, no slow tuning of eyes to a fuzzy picture of the world each morning – just a simple case of opening his eyes and taking it all in. I've had that moment described to me a hundred times and each time it sounds amazing. Graham did admittedly look like a panda for a week but a couple of black eyes is a small price to pay for what he said his surgery had given him and hey, he could now see how ridiculous he looked without the need for specs!

I can't imagine the day-to-day considerations of having to wear glasses. My eyes are failing fast though and what I *can* see is that someday soon I might very well need a pair. I suppose I could get used to keeping them close to hand for emergencies, knowing exactly where they were stowed if I planned on a spot of reading, say. But the unknowns would throw me completely. What would I do if I couldn't see without them and they were knocked off and broken on a night out? I'm sure it's happened to quite a lot of our bespectacled brethren. Would I stumble around blindly for the rest of the evening or would I have to go home straight away? Game over, no fun, sent off home like a blind Billy No Mates? Boo.

Maybe I could stay out, but how much fun would I really have in a noisy watering hole where only up-close lip-reading would make sense of the my drunken friends? And then getting home? Catching a cab? Feeling my way into the road like some sightless zombie only to be mowed down by a speeding yob I could only hear roaring towards me? Nightmare! No thanks.

What if I needed glasses for driving but sat on them by mistake at the services, hundreds of miles from home? What would I do? Take my chances with nose pressed against the windscreen at ten miles per hour or hitchhike home and hope I don't get strangled?

What can now be done to take the peril out of all of those seemingly innocuous but potentially terrifying scenarios is to me just astounding. The friend who smelt her eyes being seared told me that one of the true joys of having her sight restored was that for the first time, on train journeys she could actually make out the animals grazing in the fields she was whizzing by. She'd never bothered to look out of the window before and never stopped to question what those indistinct white blobs were on the blurry green plain outside. Now she marvels at what she knows to be sheep whenever she travels. Brilliant.

I've read of procedures with mini electronic cameras that have 'cured' permanent blindness, too. That just blows my mind. And of course it is not just eyes that have benefitted from the wonders of modern medicine. Fertility drugs are making it possible for people who would make the very best of parents to have a go at giving the gift of life for themselves. Once a child is conceived, 4-D scans now provide a window on the womb that shows Junior in all his / her glory! A friend of a friend even swore that their baby was waving to them when they went for a 4-D scan. Amazing.

Transplants happen every day to prolong and improve life, with organs harvested from donors or even shared by living loved ones. Nothing goes to waste – how very modern and thrifty. People the world over are having their hearing restored or improved and I doubt there's a sense or bodily function known to us that hasn't had some wonder drug tailored to it for the sake of life's enrichment. Where once certain symptoms were a sure sign of imminent death, nowadays they can be knocked on the head with a visit to the doctor and a quick gargle of something not altogether unpleasant.

The blind can see again, those who have lost limbs can walk again – or indeed dance their way around celebrity ice rinks on television! We can walk on the Moon and float in Space. We can change the weather at will as they did at the Beijing Olympics and stay in touch all around the planet with no need for the oracles of folk lore, just a little BlackBerry will do. At this rate we'll be turning water into wine with a couple of tablets we can just plink, plink, fizz into a jug filled from the tap! (By the way, I'd like a cut of any proceeds should this idea ever take off in future – soluble tablets that turn water into wine; consider it copyrighted, it was my idea first and I want at least twenty per cent of the profits if

Theo 'Dragon' Paphitis (also represented by my agent) takes it on!)

Anyway, moving on from the miracles of Man and modern medicine I have to report that it is in fact my father who has made the latest great discovery to define our times. Whilst beavering away in his tardis at home, my dad unwittingly unlocked the very secrets of time travel! I kid you not, my very own 'Dad Who' recently reported that he had stumbled across a modern day means of making time itself stand still!

As part of his birthday present I'd bought Dad a Sky Plus satellite package with all the gadgets and gizmos. He's a massive sports fan and there's nothing he likes more than watching the cricket while Mum's over digging in the allotment. It would be safe to say that my dad is not particularly up on modern technology so I had the Sky box and everything else all put in and set up for him. Having not heard from him, I assumed that all was working well with his new toy. However, a few days later he asked me a question that revealed his new discovery.

He took me to one side, and rather sweetly revealed, 'Jem, the other day I was watching India versus Pakistan when the doorbell rang.' Having established that my mother was nowhere to be seen – door answering is her department in their world but she was probably 'out the back' fetching them both some afternoon cake! – he took the bull by the horns, pressed 'pause' on the live TV feed and went to see who had called. Apparently he was required to drop some keys back to the local church, so he skipped out for five minutes before returning to his game. It was then that his conundrum over the space–time continuum revealed itself.

On screen was a '-5' graphic that showed how much time out of the live game he had missed whilst the system was paused. He picked up from where he'd left off, finished watching the game but couldn't help wondering what the rest of the world had done with the five minutes they had had whilst he was down at the church. This problem perplexed him to the point where he felt compelled to ask.

'Jem, I'm now five minutes behind the rest of the world, how am I ever going to catch that time up? My watch doesn't tell the right time now does it?' Priceless, I love that man!

There is nothing so heart-warming for me as seeing my dad embrace the new technological wonders of our age. The man who felt that the TV had prolonged his life by five minutes has form in this field. When I first got him a mobile phone I could never get through to him on it. When I asked why, he explained that he never switched it on because he was scared the battery would run out! Worse, he said he'd never hear it ring anyway as he'd stowed it safely away in the glove compartment of his car, all wrapped up in a towel 'so it doesn't get bashed.' With comments like that it's not hard to see why it took him thirty years to get a dishwasher!

Anyway, here we are, all hurrying around the world, modern miracles taking place everywhere we turn and my dear old dad just five minutes behind. In a world where economies are collapsing, the polar ice caps melting, wars are raging and everyone's moaning – sometimes none more so than me, I confess – I thought it about time a note of optimism was sounded to cut through all the doom and gloom. The human race has much it can do to strive to be better but sometimes it is important to stop and remember the good we've done. Clearly the Good Lord still has his work cut out to try and save us from ourselves but it's nice to know that in some quarters we're doing our bit to lighten his load . . . from curing the blind to helping some of the flock to walk again. We really have, through our ingenuity and perseverance, made a few miracles an accessible reality for millions of people. That to me is amazing and it's clear to see the possibilities are endless – for me, for you, for everyone and even my dad, old Father Time himself – the man convinced he made the world stand still at the touch of a button!

22

Swimming with Sharks

When was the last time you genuinely could not believe what you were seeing on TV? I'm not talking about natural disasters, superhuman feats or weird, oddball programming. I mean when was the last time you were watching something you thought just should not be allowed on the nation's screens?

More than a few out there might think that my own show fits that bill perfectly. They're entitled to their opinion of course, but for numerous reasons, as I have explained over the past few years, they are wrong! I don't want to re-open that particular can of worms but I couldn't dismiss the genuine astonishment I felt recently, without seeing if anyone else out there is as incensed as I was.

I was going about my usual mid-morning business during a school holiday, juggling three kids from one arm to the next, pulling laps in a never-ending race around the house, taking phone calls, arranging meetings and wondering aloud why some bright spark hasn't yet made an attachment that would fix a mop to my backside without causing too much discomfort. You might smile but the miles I clock up chasing hyperactive toddlers round and round could actually be put to some good use. I could get a start on the housework. Imagine the cleaning I'd get done if I could easily clip a mop onto my tailbone for the endless games of chase my little princesses love me to play with them. The floor would be spick-and-span in no time.

Anyway, it was on an 'ordinary' (for ordinary, read 'manic') day like this that I stumbled across something on TV that genuinely shocked me to my core. There, bold as brass on mid-morning TV, was an advert for Quick Quid, a short-term loan provider offering to plug that horrible gap that arrives each month between paydays, when the last pay cheque is spent and the next one still some way off. All quite straightforward I thought, at first glance. There's been a fair few times in the past where I've asked for an advance to enable me to make ends meet. In these gloomy economic times, I reasoned that there were probably quite a few who would look to rely on the sort of bridging loan that Quick Quid were offering. It wasn't until the slick advert had nearly played out that I did a double take. There on screen was the interest rate such a loan would set its customers back. 'Typcial APR *2356* per cent' it said! Bloody hell, I thought.

Even the most pricey credit cards don't go much above thirty per cent so 2356 per cent annual interest is truly astronomical. And presumably for many of the people they are targeting, damn near unaffordable. I have read about and been in fervent support of measures to clamp down on unscrupulous loan sharks preying on the vulnerable in poor areas, but here, on national TV, was an advert seducing viewers with the promise of easy cash but at a small-print rate of interest that is surely every bit as crippling as anything charged by a burly bruiser from the estate. Worse, when I logged on to Quick Quid's website to double check for the sake of my disbelieving eyes I found this little kick in the teeth: 'Finance charge will be between £10 and £14.75 per £50 borrowed.' Ouch.

Now, I don't dispute that Quick Quid are a reputable company that operates within the law and according to all the guidelines the government sets in the troublesome area of lending. I also concede that they have probably helped out a great many people whose cash had stopped flowing temporarily, getting them through a lean couple of days until their own money came trickling back in. I don't know how they go about checking on their potential customers, their ability to repay or even if it is in the best interests of their applicants to sign up to what Quick Quid offer. I don't think, though, that they resort to thuggery and the sorts of strong-arm tactics favoured by bully-boy lenders, criminals that have made miserable the lives of so many in this country who just wanted to borrow a bit of cash to tide their families over. But where the bully-boys have got involved, tales are wide-spread of people being coerced into all sorts, even prostitution to pay back 'in kind' some of the cash they have borrowed. One lady I read about ended up paying a loan shark neighbour £88,000 to cover what started out as a £1,500 loan. Exorbitant interest rates spiralled and what started out as a comparatively small debt became a black hole from which she would never have escaped without police intervention.

As I say, Quick Quid are a perfectly legal business offering a perfectly straightforward service to potential customers. They don't deny the costs involved in borrowing from them and don't hide from them either but that to me is not the point. At this time of all times, bang in the middle of the worst economic crisis since the war, surely the government should be reining in advertising of this sort. They rightly splash big warnings on the front of cigarette packets, shouldn't they do something similar with nationally broadcast adverts encouraging millions of hard-pressed Britons to get into a debt they might never be able to repay? Fair enough if the APR was even vaguely affordable but 2356 per cent? Come off it.

Correct me if I'm wrong, but this country's economic meltdown was partly brought on by us all borrowing wildly beyond our means. Personal debt boomed as the house-buying bubble mushroomed. Then a bust, the likes of which we were promised by Gordon Brown had been abolished, arrived and the emphasis, we were told, had to shift back towards saving. We had all become drunk on limitless lending and the credit cards aplenty we had all accrued were maxed out. We were 'all in this together' according to the Tories and an 'Age of Austerity' beckoned. The nation's belt had to be tightened and individually we had to shake off the hangover brought on by the excesses of the past ten years and come blinking back to a sobriety that would be built on prudent saving for the future, not reckless borrowing for the present. With this in mind, and this country's finances at crisis point, I find it frankly unbelievable that we can sanction adverts for companies that will surely sucker even more people into debts they might never be able to pay back.

There are millions of people genuinely desperate for money in this country and this sort of advertising surely just preys on them. For everyone else it simply plays to the 'if-you-want-it-you-can-have-it-even-if-you-can't-afford-it' mentality fostered during Brown's boom years, which was meant to be over now. Even for those out there who are foregoing the luxuries of life and just need this cash to survive, I have to ask if this is the best way.

Apparently last year a million people used their credit card to draw out cash that they then used to meet monthly mortgage payments. They too would have been charged crazy rates of interest to do so, surely storing up yet more problems for the following month.

Up and down the country, thousands are chipping out bridgework and flocking to flog their gold jewellery to companies who advertise all day on TV. It is estimated that in 2009 thirty-five tonnes of bullion was salvaged from scrap gold, that's £700 million pounds' worth! And yet certain companies have offered as little as 9% of the real value of the gold sent to them. Some people are calling it a fool's gold rush, and they might have a point.

This is allowed to go on without any government warning or advice. At a time when people need help to make the most of what assets they have, companies have been allowed to swoop in and rip off a public that should be better protected by our politicians. Given the balls-up Gordon Brown made of selling the country's gold reserves, you might think that the moment was right for the government to make amends. Surely they could set up a similar scheme offering better rates of return than the outfits out there, and make a little bit on the side for the taxpayer, too.

In 2008, two hundred thousand people apparently fell victim to loan sharking in the UK, to the tune of a collective £30 million debt. I see no reason why the government can't intervene here too. Why can't they set up some loans at reasonable rates of interest to those hardest hit by the recession? If the need is genuine and we're talking about nappies for babies and food in mouths, not the latest game on the Playstation, why can't the State step in and help out? We've bailed out rich bankers with billions, £30 million for some hard-pressed voters seems like small beer in comparison.

Whatever the way to go, I'm sure it can't be via televised adverts luring people into loans at thousands of per cent APR. That can only add to a problem we were all meant to be fixing, and a culture we were meant to be changing together. We're all cutting our cloth according to the prevailing times and people everywhere should be staying within their means, and indeed looking to build on them through saving, not blowing them through fast 'I-deserve-it-now' living. I really believe the government could and should do more for those who are starved of cash and have no other option but even if they can't help from the public purse, they could start at least by taking away the temptation being beamed endlessly into homes each and every day. They know as well as I do that if you're worried about drowning in a sea of debt the last thing you should do is go swimming with sharks.

23

A Bridge Too Far?

If you have teeth as bad as mine it doesn't pay to be scared of the dentist. When I look in the mirror it frequently seems like a bag of smashed crockery is smiling back at me. I have been whipped in and out of the dentist's chair more times than an England footballer before Euro '96. I'll soon be going back for some more work on the fangs that are falling apart in my head, and where normally a trip to see the man with the mouth drill wouldn't bother me, now I'm not so sure. Not after last time . . .

My mother was always quite strict about us going to the dentist when we were kids. Unfortunately I was a lot less strict with myself about doing everything she told us was for the best. I didn't get the brace I should have had in my youth – hence the aforementioned fangs I now sport – and I couldn't be bothered with regular check-ups in my twenties – hence all the problems I've stored up for myself now! I've basically got to sort my whole mouth out before I go to America for meetings about taking my show over there and after years of neglect on my part, there is much to be done. A few years ago I began the remedial work required with a long overdue visit to the dentist. My experience with him left me in no doubt about the scale of the task.

My memories of what was, to that point at least, just a regular Saturday afternoon are patchy, up until the moment where the dentist had actually, physically mounted me! From there on, the images are seared into my brain. Literally on top of me with beads of sweat tumbling from his forehead into my mouth, he was a man possessed. Angry as he looked, he had no problem with me – he was just trying to dislodge the remnants of one of my shattered teeth. At one point I thought he was going to put a foot either side of my head as he tried to heave his quarry out of my face. He looked like a mad farmer trying to pull a stubborn turnip.

When he was done with pulling he brought out a range of tools that looked like they belonged at a blast furnace plant. He began digging and drilling and then finally, welding! I was terrified, staring wide-eyed at the nurses whilst strangely, completely numbed of all pain. There was so much I could see and yet so little I could feel, all I could do was dart my eyes from nurse to dentist and back again in confusion. As he melted and fused bits of my jaw back together, plumes of smoke rose out of my clamped-open mouth. He could have started a bonfire in there for all I know!

Thankfully all was well that ended well. We had taken a step in the right direction, whatever he had fixed he had done without hurting me but the dentist did warn me that the repair job I needed was only half-started. After all the time I'd gone without getting my teeth checked, there was a lot more for him to fix. I arranged a second appointment.

Unfortunately, work commitments always conspired to make it nigh-on impossible to fit that second appointment into my schedule. The dental work needed to be done though so I arranged an emergency appointment with another dentist near where I live. Big mistake . . .

The signs were good when I first arrived. Nice, white, professionally straightened and polished smiles all around, warm handshakes and *Steve Wright* (one of my radio heroes) *In The Afternoon* being piped into the waiting room. After the introductions I was led through to the fabled chair and lowered back. I was calm at this point, I had no reason not to be and so settled back to watch a TV they had embedded in their ceiling above my head. What do you think it was showing? The ITV2 repeat of my show from that morning! I hate seeing myself on TV but I wouldn't have to worry too much about that this time. Just surviving became the order of the day.

It took twenty minutes to turn me from the coherent television presenter playing above the dentist's head to the shambling greying wreck that left him. The needle he produced to numb my gums did no such thing. Instead of locally dulling half of my face, the dentist hit a vein in my mouth and injected the anaesthetic straight into my bloodstream. I didn't know there was a problem at first but when I started feeling queasy I knew it was going to be downhill from there on.

I must have vomited about fifteen times, all over the surgery. The anaesthetic was reacting badly with everything designed to keep my insides inside whilst also making it impossible for me to get any kind of rigidity into any part of my body. I was flopping about all over the place as I repeatedly wretched. There was now nothing for it; realising his error, the dentist called for an ambulance.

I couldn't be trusted to get myself out of his third-floor surgery on my own without crashing down several flights of stairs, streaking the walls as I went in violent technicolour. The only means of transport was one of those stand-up wheeley trolleys that could just as well be used to fetch parcels from the mail room. A stretcher I could have handled but not this – where was the dignity? On a stretcher I could have closed my eyes and pretended I was knocked unconscious or in a coma or something. Instead I was strapped in and carted off like Hannibal Lecter! I was bounced down every stair from three floors up and with each jolt came the gag and need to heave some more. Not withstanding the rubbish teeth, this was not a pretty sight.

Eventually we made it to terra firma but lucky me, on the ground floor a little crowd had gathered to see who might be making use of the newly arrived ambulance parked outside. This was all I needed. Thankfully nobody asked me to pose for photos and I was loaded into the back of the ambulance to continue my vomiting, but not before some 'well-wisher' had tried to rouse the other onlookers into a football chant at my expense! Just as if he was singing proudly with his tribe at Wembley, he pointed at me and began, 'You're going home in a f**king ambulance!' Over and over. Whatever he lacked in compassion, I couldn't fault him for accuracy. Ten out of ten, I was going home in a, ahem, ambulance.

I finally did make it home after a brief stop in hospital to check that whatever I had been injected with was flushing out of my system. I had nothing left in my stomach to bring up and sure enough I started to feel a bit better by the time I'd crawled into my own bed early that evening.

The drugs had worn off, the wooziness had gone and there was no more sick left in me to come out. My first, worst and only drugs trip was over but it was not done with me yet. As soon as I got into bed at about 7 p.m. I was overwhelmed by hunger. I was starving, absolutely ravenous. I had never been hungrier in my life! I couldn't explain why, I just had to have food and so I began eating everything I could find. I filled my face non-stop until 4 a.m. the following morning, barely pausing for breath between greedily shovelled mouthfuls. I was devouring whatever I could get my hands on. Smear some ketchup on the double duvet and I would probably have started on that too. It wasn't until some days later that I realised what had happened. As Carla so helpfully pointed out, 'You were smacked off your tits, Jez, and then you went down with the munchies!' Quite.

And so, as I write I still haven't been back for the work that needs to be done on my teeth. After an ordeal like the last time, I might ordinarily try and make my excuses. However, the fact remains that it has to be done before I head off to the States. I can't very well turn up to them with a face full of ivory rubble and confirm their worst fears about us Brits not caring for dental hygiene! I have therefore had to bite as much of the bullet as I can with my ramshackle gnashers and book an appointment with the man I should have trusted all along. I am back in for what amounts to a major restoration project on a crumbling old relic. For an old country estate read 'my mouth in a right state' and they are basically gutting the place and starting again. Caps, veneers and bridges aplenty – the list is long, the cost is massive, and now the risks seem endless, too. I mean, how will it turn out? I don't know if I'll emerge flashing newly polished ivory like a Bee Gee on full beam or even if I'll emerge at all. Watch this ~~space~~ face!

24

Sympathy for a Lout

I don't know what has come over me. I know I haven't been drinking, I'm not on any drugs and everything around me is no more rosy today than it was yesterday. All that said, I am having strange feelings of compassion towards an individual who would typically inspire little more than contempt in me. Put me in front of someone who blew millions on hookers, crack cocaine and a selfish nihilistic lifestyle that alienated a whole community, if not the whole country, and I would normally feel justified in giving both barrels. For a time that was all my head was telling me to do in this case but something recently has kept tugging away at my heart strings, and it keeps compelling me to feel just a little bit sorry for the 'Lotto lout' who's blown the lot, Michael Carroll.

I, like most people, was shocked, appalled and probably more than just a little jealous when the lurid stories about the man who was dubbed 'King of the Chavs' first broke. Not long after he scooped £9.7 million on the National Lottery, the country was treated to almost daily tales of Carroll's disgusting behaviour and constant excesses.

He bought a garish mansion and played host to an endless stream of noisy, wild, drug-fuelled parties. He and his mates apparently thought nothing of using the land outside his property for loud gatherings at all hours. These were the cause of countless disputes with neighbours who were driven away from the homes they loved and the close community they felt this one selfish lout had destroyed without a single thought for anyone else.

For so long I was right with them and everyone else who condemned his behaviour. If it had been in my power back then, I would have said without hesitation, 'lock this menace up!' In fact, if I had been his neighbour I would have made a strong case for freezing his assets, too. If his new money was the root of all the criminality and anti social nuisances brought to my doorstep I would have lobbied for the authorities to take it back for safekeeping until he'd done some time and proved he had been educated to the point where he could spend it more maturely, without breaking the law or damaging the local community. And if and when it got returned to him, I would have wanted to see him monitored and put on some sort of three strikes rule. Mess up three times and the money would be fed back into the Lotto Good Causes pot. I just don't believe that money won on a public lottery should be allowed by law to be spent on illegal acts that only bring misery to public streets. If the police can sieze the assets of convicted drug barons and put them towards the common good, so they should be able to commandeer and make better use of lottery winnings willfully squandered on criminal acts.

I would still make those points now. In fact, in the case of some lottery winners, like 'Lotto Rapist' Iorworth Hoare, I'd add my voice to those who say nobody who commits such vile and violent crimes should be allowed to make *any* money from *any* sort of lottery. It surely can't be right that it still 'could be you' if you are a man who has been jailed for life for attempted rape and spent sixteen years behind bars after six previous convictions for rape, attempted rape and indecent assault. Nobody should be allowed to profit so fantastically from a game run for the people when they have so destructively, so sickeningly and so brutally taken so much from another human being.

I understand the calls from some to ban any convicted criminal from ever winning on the Lottery but that, for me, is a far harder line to draw. This one is easy. I mean, it is difficult to make the lottery operator the moral judge on whether or not a man once jailed for, say, being drunk and disorderly thirty years ago should win big or not. But we can all say simply and swiftly that convicted murderers, paedophiles and rapists should *never* ever be allowed to trouser millions from a national pastime like the Lottery. I'd make it law in a heartbeat. Even for those who could 'prove' they are completely, properly rehabilitated after years of incarceration and therapy, I'd still say 'tough!' If I had my way, for some crimes you would forfeit certain things forever and the chance to become a millionaire via the country's lottery would be one of them.

Similar things were probably said about Michael Carroll when he won. He was an idiot and a menace. But that was nothing compared to what he became when, aged just nineteen, he was given ten million to put in the bank. Thereafter he became an outright danger to society, a violent man and huge user of drugs and prostitutes.

His spending was out of control. He is said to have given away over £5 million to friends and family and spent

£200,000 on gold chains for them and himself. He then got into narcotics and spent £2,000 a day on crack cocaine as he turned his mansion into one big drug den that was open all hours for anything that was dangerous, destructive and deadly. With the lifestyle came the typical bad crowd who followed him round until the money ran out. To be honest, with all the trouble he has got into since winning his money, it is a wonder he's alive at all. Gangsters muscled their way into his inner circle with Michael either too scared or to smashed to do anything about it. I've read reports of him regularly having to pay up huge sums of money being squeezed out of him by menaces, of him being terrified of the next plot to rip him off. Much of the five million he apparently 'gave away' I wouldn't be surprised to learn had been forced out of him on pain of death.

To be fair though, no matter what you think of his subsequent behaviour, nobody would really begrudge a man in Michael's position a bit of a splurge. You may disagree that he was entitled to the money or even that the system should allow a criminal like him to win it but the fact that a broke teenage binman became a millionaire in the blink of an eye and then went spending is hardly a great surprise. Who wouldn't celebrate that? I would, and for a time at that age I may well have gone a little wild with new wealth too. To an extent I can understand a young lad living the dream. Investing in his football team (he apparently gave £1 million to Rangers!), decking out a new mansion with swimming pool, widescreens and all the boys' toys. Treating mates to holidays and parties, buying a fleet of fancy cars and even loading up on bling – I can see how a nineteen-year-old catapulted to untold riches overnight might well want to have it all, as Michael did. But soon enough I would have to listen to the good advice that I know would have been telling me that the parties had to stop some time and that the extravagances were becoming reckless indulgences. Yes, I'd have had plenty of fun but not at such a cost to my health, the law and the local community. I would have listened to the good people around me. It seems clear to me though that Michael Carroll never had many good influences, and to that extent he was an accident waiting to happen, almost an 'unfortunate' recipient of outrageous good fortune.

I'm sure Camelot make every effort to give good advice to their big winners. I'm sure that same advice was offered to Michael. He may even have taken it for a time but as I know from working on my show, it is one thing to set up help for people and to talk them through the first few steps, it is quite another for them to take up the baton and see it through to a positive conclusion for themselves.

I know we can't and that we shouldn't close the door to people from any social background winning such huge sums of money but society must at some point have a duty to intervene. We rightly step in when we think children might be in danger because of the lifestyles they are exposed to in the chaotic households some are brought up in but what about young adults who become a danger to themselves through a freakish slice of good fortune?

Michael Carroll's problems seem so predictable to me. He never seemed likely to grasp the need to use his wealth in a way that didn't have a profoundly negative impact – for himself as much as anyone else. And I can't get away from it, there's something about his circumstances that just make me feel sorry for him. He came from a traumatic and destabilised background, suffered terribly at school with dyslexia and ADHD and was always viewed as rather limited. Believe it or not, he has done some very good work for charity in between the bouts of mindlessness but what talents he had were laid to waste like so much of the money he won.

Don't get me wrong, I don't condone any of the wrongs Michael Carroll did before, and certainly not after he won his millions. The way he so flagrantly flouted the law should probably have seen him jailed, and for a lot longer than the small sentences he did pick up for affray and cocaine possession. I am not decrying the system either, and definitely not the Lottery, just wondering aloud whether it wouldn't have been better for everyone if this apparent good luck had actually passed Michael Carroll by.

Some would say there was a poetic justice to the fact that Michael was later run out of his own dream home, chased away by some of the thugs and vultures who bullied and extorted from him. He was a bully himself, he made his neighbours' lives a misery – an eye for an eye, right? Well no, not for me, not on this one. Michael was forcibly evicted from his house by the same people who apparently killed his five dogs by slitting their throats. That would upset and terrify anyone.

Michael himself probably realises that winning ten million didn't do him many favours. Maybe even he would concede that my idea of taking the money back from him when it was first apparent he was going into a self-destructive, criminal spiral might in fact have been a good idea. If it had been, some might have been left now. If my three strikes idea was in place maybe Michael would have seen the deal as a sort of good behaviour bond to sign up for, one that would keep him on the straight and narrow in the same way that it would for any citizen hoping to strike it rich when buying a ticket.

The reality of his life is that he is now broke and the rollercoaster ride has come to an end. He is, unbelievably for a man with ten million pounds in the bank just seven years ago, back on benefits. Many will be up in arms about that too and as ever with Michael Carroll, it is easy to see why. I still can't shake off feeling a bit sorry for him, though. It is sad for me to see the devastating effect of too many of the pressures that come with wealth being forced upon someone who was never even nearly well equipped enough to deal with it and especially for someone who confesses he was much happier without it anyway. It brought the worst out in him and most of those around him.

I have never been a Michael Carroll fan. Some of the things he's done truly offend me and I understand that many people would think the stupendous luck that came his way was nothing but undeserved. If I'd lived anywhere near him I'd probably have wanted to throttle him, if I'd seen any one of his antisocial acts I'd probably think flogging too good for him. But I just can't get past the fact that for Michael Carroll, his life seems predestined to be at odds with the rest of the world. The family that for most of us is the basic support structure of our lives was for him a source of horrible turbulence. School, which for most of us is a springboard from which to launch into life was for him little more than constant frustration. Even the absurd good luck that might have been a passport to unimaginable fulfilment was for him just a fast track to the worst sorts of experiences that pulled apart his life.

In all honesty I doubt I'd like the man if I met him, but that doesn't stop me feeling for his plight. I feel sorry for the people he may have used, abused and bullied along the way but I'd wager that Michael has probably suffered all that and more himself – and not least since he won the Lottery. He's been rightly castigated for all he did wrong but I just get the sense that deep down with Michael Carroll there's another story to tell, one that none of us would envy, even with millions in the bank.

25

A Man More Hated Than Me?

Who is the man you most loathe in Great Britain? A quick straw poll I conducted threw up a predictable number of usual suspects. Unsurprisingly, John Terry remains highly unpopular amongst the ladies, whilst Gordon Brown and David Cameron predictably split opinion amongst pretty much everyone I asked. I didn't expect to hear a 'Jonathan Ross' but wasn't surprised to get a couple of 'Abu Hamza's and the odd 'Jim Davidson'. Most shocking was to hear the vitriol some reserved for National Treasure Sir Paul McCartney. I thought this man could do no wrong but, believe it or not, he seems to feature quite prominently on a fair few 'shit lists' out there!

It doesn't seem so long ago that I was regularly topping these lists myself. Up until recently, every time I walked into work a colleague would gleefully present the latest public rage against me! Be it a press clipping, a letter sent in or any one of a million online rants, my team took great delight in mocking my plunging popularity in some quarters. Laughter they insisted was the best medicine but for a time it was quite sobering to see just how enraged I made people I'd never even met. I am used to it now though and there's no getting away from it: a lot of the abuse directed at me is very funny! Rufus Hound once suggested that all you would find if you cut me open was 'black and wrong' and I've just watched *Mock The Week,* where Russell Howerd received rapturous applause for suggesting that Gordon Brown should decapitate me! The set up would take too long to explain here but trust me, as violent murder goes for a gag, it seemed to go down rather well!

I have long since realised I am not everyone's cup of tea and I am OK with that. I know that those who don't like me *really* don't like me. Over the last couple of years though, someone has come to the fore who even I am pretty confident is easily more detested than me. His name is Nick Griffin, MEP.

Now, you have to go pretty far to beat me in the national loathing stakes. I don't think, in fact I damn well *know,* I'm not all that bad but that is not the point. However, the fact remains that anyone with designs on becoming 'Britain's Most Hated' should know that to wrest the crown for themselves they first have to sink lower than me in the hearts and minds of everyone in this country. Looking at the occasional contents of my postbag, believe me, that won't come easy!

I'll be honest, it has never been a title I've coveted, nor one I've particularly relished, but it seems it is one I am always a leading contender for and to take it from me, someone generally has to be a dictator, despot or some sort of serial killer. Despite my lack of qualifications on those grounds, I always seemed to be in most people's Top Ten! But now, ever since Mr Griffin went on *Question Time,* there has been another pretender to the crown, right up there with me and Harold Shipman. In fact, after that appearance it would appear there's no contest. As he said himself, Nick Griffin is now 'the most loathed man in Britain!'

This is no great surprise, of course. Anyone who can spout the vile, divisive, incendiary bullshit he can, and actually believe it too, is never going to last long in the affections of most right-thinking people in this country. As he found out shortly after his much-touted arrival on Britain's flagship political debate show, his views provoke little but disgust in the majority of the electorate he insists should vote for his BNP. Even before he got into the studio that day there were near riots outside the BBC, such is the outrage he provokes wherever he goes and whenever he speaks.

The wider debate surrounding his *Question Time* debut concerned whether or not he should have been allowed to appear at all. Those defending argued that the BNP now had some democratically elected representatives courtesy of the last round of European elections and therefore had a right to be heard alongside other parties whose parliamentarians had been voted for by the British people. Those against said any appearance would legitimise an illegally constituted party, give publicity and an ill-deserved platform to someone accused of being little more than a racist. I understood both arguments at the time but the fact is he appeared. The show went ahead and Nick Griffin had his say. That can't be changed but the fallout from it still reverberates today.

In just under an hour Nick Griffin decried homosexuals kissing as 'creepy' and, ignoring the cultural diversity that helps make this country so Great, hinted that any followers of Islam were never likely to fit in with fundamental British values. The audience gave him a fair old battering with one member even suggesting that perhaps it was Nick Griffin and his like who should leave Britain, preferably for Antarctica where he could enjoy an all white, 'colourless' landscape for ever more! Brilliant. That was not just democracy in action but British democracy. There's nobody quite like the British to take *their* right to free speech and throw it back in the faces of bigots who abuse it. I love our propensity to take the piss and give those who deserve it the proverbial bloody nose. Nick Griffin got his amidst a hostile atmosphere that was never going to be anything but a 'bear pit'.

A lot of people had wanted to take down Nick Griffin and all he stands for, for a very long time. The audience, a slice of Nick's prospective electorate, did that job admirably. There was no sliming out of anything with them. The wiggle room he creates for himself in the press was squeezed from him via the immediacy of debate. Faced with past quotes extracted from some of his more repulsive rhetoric he had nowhere to run. Faced with a live audience he needed to convince, the normal wriggling just gave way to what looked like squirming.

Having said what he said and campaigned for what he has throughout his political career, *Question Time* was always going to be a tough gig for Nick Griffin. And so it should have been. But I just wish the programme makers, and his fellow panellists, had let him dig a bigger hole for himself. The hype surrounding his appearance hit fever pitch beforehand and it was clear from the off that most of the political heavyweights sat alongside him could not wait to be the one who landed the killer blow. Moreover, they were all so desperate to be the one that connected with *the* question or *the* comment to floor him that I actually think they may even have helped him a little towards achieving his aims.

Left to his own devices, Nick Griffin tends to hang himself with his own words. Most of us can see within about two seconds of him opening his mouth what rot he is speaking. However, on *Question Time*, while there was plenty from him which rightly drew indignation from all of us watching, too often it seemed as though the focus of the show was all on Nick Griffin and who would be quickest to the front of the queue to attack him. At times it might almost have seemed as if his fellow panellists were ganging up on him – and that, unfortunately, will have played right into his hands.

They tried to goad the personality rather than letting his opinions and policies die on their arse for themselves. Left to speak freely, Mr Griffin tied himself in knots, ran out of steam or just repulsed those who came to scrutinise him. I believe the damage done to the BNP would have been far greater if the *Question Time* team had encouraged Griffin to speak more about his outrageous policies. As it was, with everyone falling over themselves to get to him and at him, even with good reason, the trashing of the BNP they desired may have been rather less than they achieved. And certainly far less than Nick Griffin deserved.

The right-thinking majority will have been disgusted by him, but they were disgusted before and will be to the end of time. What about those on the fringes? What about those disillusioned with politics and politicians in the wake of all the scandals of recent years? In a moment of supreme irony, some of those people might have viewed the man who some say is the biggest most bilious bully of them all as being a victim of bullying himself! To come to the end of a programme where someone's whole philosophy could and should have been exposed, to enable a man like Nick Griffin the opportunity to cry foul and claim unfair treatment borders on the criminal.

Thankfully, away from this sideshow, the courts of this land have triumphed where many a political debater has not. And they have hit Nick Griffin where it hurts – right in the ballots! The BNP has now had its membership policy declared illegal. They were essentially constituted as a 'whites-only' party but now they have been forced by law to accept members from every ethnic background. Superb! Granted, it will be a very brave person from a minority background who knocks on the door to be the first to sign up, but a 'secret millionaire' from Stoke insists he wants to be the first. Mo Chaudry says he wants to infiltrate the BNP, join up and 'find out what makes them tick'. Ultimately he wants to expose them, and good luck to him. Just imagine if Mo was the first of thousands of Brits of every colour, who signed up en masse with the BNP. Within days they could call an emergency meeting and vote out everyone who was racist, intolerant or in any other way 'un-British' as most of us known the term. They could oust Nick Griffin and anyone who supports him from the party's leadership in one fell swoop. How good would that be?

Cast out from legitimacy by his own re-shaped party (a British National Party that was truly representative of a modern Great Britain), Nick Griffin might lose the oxygen of his publicity and fade from the political landscape. Out of sight and out of mind, he may one day have to relinquish his claim to be the most loathed man in Britain. That title might then swing back to me . . . but under those terms I'd take it gladly and crack open the bubbly to celebrate!

26

Life Really is Unfair!

How many times were you told as a child that 'life is unfair'? How many times as a parent have you played that conversational top trump yourself? It really is some moment when you first hear yourself utter the immortal words that stopped you in your tracks when complaining to your own parents thirty years earlier.

I always had a burning sense of injustice if Mum or Dad nipped my fun in the bud by telling me that, yes, life was unfair. Now I know that a broken promise to play cricket in the garden or a deal undone to take the kids to the cinema is sometimes unavoidable when the iniquities of the adult world rear up to make a mockery of a family's best laid plans. If Daddy has to go to work unexpectedly he has to go, no matter the earlier guarantee to put himself forward for a thrashing on the Wii. If the kids have to put some sensible clothes on to go outdoors, that is what they will be doing, regardless of whether or not they want to brave the elements wearing only wellies and some princess wings! (Trust me, I have had this argument with two of my daughters!) We do what we have to, they do as they are told and if that seems unfair to either of us, well that is because it probably is.

I don't carry the rage I once felt when things went unfairly against me, but I still keep an eye out for the little inequalities that life throws up. Obviously I am no longer the little boy trying to understand why he is not getting his own way. Now I am a grown man wondering how it can be that I seem to get my own way so often, and so often without asking!

A friend of mine who worked in the music business once complained to me that the most unfair thing about his line of work was being made to attend parties for album launches and suchlike. I thought that would be the best bit for a twenty-something but he was adamant they were nothing more than expensive wastes of time that proved to him all over again just how unfair life really was.

He told me that he and his fellow low-paid lackeys would normally have to queue outside with moody bouncers while The Band were whisked straight from limo to VIP lounge. Once inside, he and his lower-league colleagues would be forced to watch while The Band and a coterie of senior executives with enough clout to get close to them were treated to endless buckets of free champagne. As they swilled back the bubbles with gay abandon my friend would join seven-deep queues at the bar before paying ten pounds a pop for a bottle of warm beer! In short, he argued against the unfairness that saw those with most getting a free ride whilst he and his mates were obliged to pay through the nose to turn out in support. He could not understand how millionaire rock stars got everything for nothing while those in tow with not two pennies to rub together got burgled every time they went to the bar. Those who could afford it didn't have to pay, those who couldn't, did!

I had to agree with him that it was totally unfair. Life is and it doesn't get any fairer the older you get, and whatever the industry you work in. For example, everything that my friend told me about his time working for a music company could equally apply to anyone working in television. There is unfairness everywhere, with the have-lots getting freebies left right and centre while so many of the have-nots they work with get next to nothing! I can see the unfairness and understand the complaints of everyone who rails against it but I won't start complaining myself. Why not? Well, sometimes nowadays I get to have a go on the gravy train myself! How unfair is that!

Is there anyone in this country who doesn't love a bargain? No. Is there any better bargain than getting something you want for nothing? No. So don't judge me for doing what any one of you would, given half the chance. I don't ask for the freebies I sometimes now receive, nor do I seek them, but I am equally not going to turn this stuff down. Neither would you, no way – read on.

My first taste of the Great Television Freebie came courtesy of the lovely Fern Britton. She was holding my hand through some of my first ridiculous attempts at presenting a couple of live episodes of *This Morning* and one day we were doing an item on some jewellery. There were a couple of diamond necklaces that had been donated to the programme and I was told that they didn't need to be sent back to the shop from whence they came.

Fern guided us expertly through the piece and at the end just turned to me and said that I should take one of the necklaces home for Carla. It was all part of the 'perks of the job' she told me, so I pocketed the shimmering piece and took it home at the end of filming. Carla was overjoyed, I thought I'd had a right result and nobody mentioned it ever again. I had half-expected to see my face on *Crimewatch* as the most brazen jewel thief in history, doing it there and then on live TV, but it seemed that Fern was right. The necklaces were presents and were now ours to enjoy! Nobody batted an eyelid. We were not the Bonny and Clyde of daytime TV, lifting loot before an audience of millions, I was just accepting a gift in a way that I was told happens all the time.

In fairness, I'm not sure the 'diamonds' in the necklace are diamonds per se – probably more likely cubic zirconia – and in the five years that have followed, the only equipment ever likely to be donated on my show is a DNA or lie detector test and I don't need one of them, thank you very much!

I'm pretty sure that sort of 'help yourself to what we're filming' is very common. In other production offices there are always perfumes and toys and beers and clothes being sent through for various teams' considerations. More than a few books or DVDs arrive too, and many of them make their way home if they're not needed for shows. Production staff benefit from this booty as much if not more than any presenter but if you really want to see life in the present giving stakes at its most unfair, the fabled goody bag is where it's at.

For these it is usually a case of celebrities only. Yep, just for turning up to quaff a few free glasses of champagne at an awards ceremony, many showbiz types are coming to expect that they will head home with a goody bag for their troubles. Award tucked under one arm, the bag dangling from the other might contain vouchers for days at spas, watches, bouquets of flowers, jewellery, expensive fragrances and all sorts of other treasure that is never asked for before-hand but bloody lovely to take home afterwards! I get to hear about more than I actually experience those extrava-gances but that is not to say I have not had my unfair share. I have been given iPod speakers I don't know what to do with, free meals in restaurants, free upgrades on flights and lapped all of them up gratefully. Who wouldn't – it's great.

People in this business will often claim that they remain unchanged by fame, success, position or privilege. I have done the self-same thing in this very book but while I think my morals, my outlook and sense of grounding have remained the same, my love of some of the little luxuries in life has definitely come on lately. Before, I just never knew how the other half lived but, unfair as it, I am now sometimes invited to have myself a first-hand glimpse. Every celebrity I know, no matter how grounded and resistant to change, in fact every person I know, no matter their wealth, background or social status would accept a better seat on a plane if they were offered it. A free meal or a great deal for no other reason than being who they are and where they are then and there will never get turned down – by anyone. And I'm no different.

I couldn't quite believe it when I walked up to check in for a flight a little while back. I was going through the usual rigmarole with the tickets, passports, etc. just like everybody else, Carla and kids in tow, when some official looking bloke appeared out of nowhere behind the counter. He stopped the check-in attendant in her tracks, scooped up my papers and pulled me to one side. He had basically recognised me, checked to make sure with a sneaky peak at my passport and then insisted I follow him to this special lounge. The lift opened up to an opulent club where everybody relaxed and helped themselves to free drinks and a lovely spread of free posh nibbles at the buffet. He ordered me and my family to relax here, with TVs to one side, computers to the other, a shower at the back and a massage if we needed it! Wow – I'd never seen anything like it and a little voice at the back of my head told me that the fact I was getting this all for nothing was very unfair . . .

Back outside, a lift ride away from this oasis of pampered calm was a maddening throng of people all jostling to get baggage checked and boarding passes printed for a flight they'd have to fight to make on time. There were kids screaming, parents stressing and all around, tense people starting their holidays with that typically British march to the bar for the first pint, even though it was only 6 a.m.

I know I didn't deserve the good fortune I was being invited to wallow in. In all *fairness* I should have gone back and said so. I hadn't paid for this and had clearly only been looked after in this way because someone had spotted a face they knew from the telly. I *should* have gone up to the man and said 'thanks but no thanks.' I *should* have gone back to take my rightful place in the queues downstairs and struggled with everyone else to steer buckled trolleys and knackered children on to a busy plane. I *should* have done this and so much more in the name of fairness, but did I? OF COURSE NOT! This was brilliant, this was the stuff of dreams – it was everything I never knew air travel could be. I loved it, I took it, and so would you!

Recently, the mere mention of my name down the phone resulted in me achieving what the Great British Taxpayer has so conspicuously failed to do in the past couple of years: I actually managed to get some of the bank's money into my pocket! Well, my daughter's actually.

Hattie is now living in Sydney. She is getting ready to go to university there and has no plans to return home anytime soon. She first travelled Down Under with her ex-boyfriend but their relationship foundered as many young loves do and about a year ago they decided to split and go their own way. At the time, Hattie owed him some money so she wrote a fifty-quid cheque and thought nothing more of it. It transpired that after he returned home, her ex lost the cheque but then found and cashed it about a year later, at just about the time I am now writing about it, in fact.

When the cheque was cashed, Hattie had £40 in her account. Lloyds, her bank, paid the cheque, pushing Hattie £10 overdrawn – a privilege for which they charged her the princely sum of £15! Since Hattie was overseas and had granted nobody back home the power of attorney over her affairs, the bank decided to send a letter to her next of kin. They wrote to explain that she was overdrawn, that they had charged her as above and furthermore that they were going to apply a further £6 per day levy for each day that she remained overdrawn, up to a maximum of £60. Let's do the sums.

	£40 credit
MINUS	£50 cheque
MINUS	£15 overdraft fee
MINUS	£60 in daily overdraft fees
Equals	£85 debit

Yep, all in all, a fifty-pound cheque my daughter had written in good faith a year earlier, when there were sufficient funds in her account, had now caused her to be a total of eighty-five pounds overdrawn! In fairness to Hattie, she did try to resolve things at her end but kept wasting what little money she had with futile phone calls from Down Under to British call centres, which were all predictably unable to help. She sounded like she needed a break so I offered to call her branch from home. Being in the right hemisphere, in fact just living down the road from it, it seemed the least I could do.

Hattie could not have been more delighted that I did. I'm sure there are a few people out there who will once more lament life's interminable unfairness but hey, life as we have established *is* unfair! I got all the money back, and more besides, without even asking for a penny!

All I did when put through was give my name as asked. I might as well have said, 'Hi, I'm Anne Robinson from *Watchdog* and I'm not leaving until I've got someone's head on a stick!' There was all manner of busying, shuffling and clicking as calls were put through back and forth until I landed in the ear of a big cheese who sounded like he'd drawn the short straw. This man, I think, was the manager and he sounded like he was about to go into a meltdown brought on by over-politeness.

I had rung him fully expecting to have to apologise for my daughter's slightly lackadaisical approach to current account management but it was he who came over all profuse. He could not have been nicer nor more understanding. Perhaps he thought I was about to drag a camera crew down to confront him, maybe he thought I was taping the call for my colleagues in the Manchester newsrooms. Hopefully he had just come to appreciate the exorbitant charges being fired at a student on the other side of the world for the shameful, opportunistic disgrace they were. Whatever the reasons, within about five minutes this man had wiped all outstanding charges and for about a tenner he allowed me to close the account on Hattie's behalf, too. Job done, no fuss and no bother. I'm not sure his shareholders would agree with his actions that day, but seeing as the British taxpayer still has quite a sizeable stake in the bank, I'm prepared to give him the benefit of the doubt and let this one slide, on our behalf. How very unfair.

The charges he had applied were unfair to begin with but the fact that my calling got them lifted when most people would have been dragged kicking and screaming to the bank to pay them is just as bad, if not worse. This man could not have been nicer but I suspect he would not have been as nice to others, and certainly not so accommodating, as he was to me. He responded to a name and perhaps even a reputation that he knew from the television and wanted to ensure I knew there was no problem with his bank and the brand. The tone he used with me was not the one that had previously been barked at my daughter but hey-ho, I took what was belatedly on offer from them, however unfair, because it helped my daughter out of a hole. Who wouldn't do the same thing in that situation?

I'll say again, I don't go looking for special favours and equally I know that it is unfair that, just because I'm on the telly, I sometimes get asked to indulge myself in them. There are many people more deserving out there. Doctors, nurses, charity workers and a million other people besides could all probably warrant the comfy seat in business class more than me but really, honestly, would you say no if it got offered to you? Life really is unfair but when that unfairness goes your way, few out there will find any reason to complain. If your team wins a match with a penalty that should never have been given, it's wry smiles all round. If you get a ticket to an Ashes Test match you would never have been able to see were it not for the fact that you host a TV show, it's wide smiles all round. I'm sorry that's unfair, but what would you do?

27

Paws for Thought:
It's Heavy, Petting

Great Britain may well be a nation of animal lovers but it does not always follow that those of us who own pets are necessarily that good at looking after them. I must confess I am not an instinctive animal lover and have always been a reluctant keeper of pets. However, with an army of young children all bleating at different times that they want to bring some hairy critter into the house, I have found myself caving in and putting up with various four-legged lodgers for their sakes.

I don't have anything against animals, it is more a case of just not trusting them. I mean, take dogs. How can you be sure about any creature that says hello to a friend by sniffing its arse? Imagine if we did that. Imagine if the minute you introduced me to your partner I popped round the back and buried my nose in his or her backside. It's just not right!

I think my mistrust of dogs must partially be inherited from my father. Whether by nature or nurture I just don't know, but from an early age I was always pretty freaked out by any encounter with a canine. Dogs seem to know they can abuse me, just as they did my dad. He said he lost count of the times he had his knee gangbanged by the corgis during his years of royal service! On one occasion he made to bow to the Queen Mother just as a corgi had mounted his shin. Head bowed and down on one knee, his respectful display towards Her Majesty was wrecked by him being nose-to-nose with one of her excited, panting hounds. They tormented him regularly but whereas the corgis seemed to be turned on by my Old Man, in my life it is a case of all dogs just turning on me.

They like to intimidate me and they can sense my fear whenever I'm around. As a child I used to resist going to play in the park. Even in later life, a leisurely promenade through the park never much appealed because I knew, just knew, that my romantic, relaxing walk would be spoiled by some dog that would snap and snarl at me until I was pinned up against a tree.

I suppose on some level I have never properly got over an early assault by a dog. It attacked as I sat in my pushchair as a child. I don't remember much about it but I have always been told that the slight scar on my forehead came from the dog that bit me that day. Ever since, I have generally conceded the upper hand whenever I've been forced into the same room as any member of the species.

So, as you can imagine, I would have been happy never to have welcomed a pet into my home. For a man as obsessed with cleanliness and hygiene as I am, the endless mountains of fur and other pet-produced matter really is too much to handle. However, if I say 'No' and Carla says 'Yes' she normally wins. And if one of the kids has rallied her to their cause the game is as good as over for me. This was the case when my darling children decided that we were to invest in a family dog. Great! They took care to buy the most fluffy and docile one they could find, so as not to scare Daddy, but even so, the thing was a menace. 'Lottie' was a bichon frise, full of love and life. She also just happened to be full of crap. She left me little welcome piles of the stuff every-where. And worse for me, every time I went to put on one of my suits for work the thing was covered in stray white hairs. To my over-obsessive eye, thanks to Lottie I looked like a polar bear every time I stepped out of the house.

In fairness, I did warm to the dog over time and as is typical of young children who grow bored of new 'toys', my kids lost interest and I was the one who ended up spending most time with it. Even more typically, just as I'd developed a proper bond with the only dog never to have bullied me, I was forced into letting her go! I was genuinely starting to really like Lottie. It was a breakthrough for me on quite a few levels. But when Carla got pregnant with our youngest, Henry, she developed an allergy to our dog pretty much overnight. Eventually the sneezing became too much, and especially with me working away so often, a new home had to be found for Lottie. At around this time, a kindly old lady we knew in a local village had lost a similar dog. She wanted another one for company and the minute she saw Lottie she fell in love with her. Problem solved – everyone happy. I felt a little put out at first but now I'm over it. One look at some of the yellow patches I'm sure I can still see on the carpet is all I need to know that ultimately Lottie leaving was probably for the best! However, my respite from the animals set to invade my house in the coming years is bound to be brief. The kids are growing up and it won't be long before I'm forced back down to Petworld on their behalf.

I remember my eldest, Hattie, when she first wanted a guinea pig. She was about seven at the time and I promised that when I went down to see her for a weekend at my parents we would all go out together and get her that first furry friend. It didn't take long for Hattie to find the pig of choice – a champagne-coloured ball of fun she was determined to call Bubbles. The purchase was textbook dad-with-daughter stuff. She cooed endlessly about the lovely Bubbles whilst I shelled out for cage, straw, bottle and wheel to go with it, not really understanding what the fuss regarding guinea pigs was all about. Hattie was going to keep her new pet at my house – not her grandparents' – so we arranged to come back in a fortnight to meet up as a family before I then drove me, Hattie and Bubbles back home.

A few days before Bubbles was due to be collected, I got a call from the pet store. It was November and temperatures were plummeting. This was not normally a problem for the store's guinea pigs as they tended to huddle together for warmth. They hadn't lost one to the cold yet, I was promised. However, Bubbles had perished. They assured me it wasn't the cold so much as the huddle that had done for poor Bubbles. Apparently Bubbles was at the bottom of a huge guinea pig pile and was crushed to death! I'm not sure I believed that – they'd probably just sold it – but the net result was that I had an excited daughter looking forward to picking up her guinea pig, and now no guinea pig. My dad stepped in to save the day.

As only he can, he tenderly employed a little artistic licence, took Hattie to one side and wove a white lie he thought was for the best. Not wanting to see Hattie crushed, he could not tell her that Bubbles was! Instead he concocted a story about guinea pigs shedding their fur and changing colour to cope with the different weather in winter. This, he explained, was why Bubbles would not now be champagne coloured, but more like a deep chocolatey brown – which just happened to be the nearest to a champagne-coloured guinea pig the pet store could find. Hattie seemed to buy the story and we all went home happy.

At the time, I was a typical single dad and was about to get used to how all my kids would be with their various pets. Hattie loved Bubbles throughout but increasingly I was the one who had to go out to the garden and clean out its cage. Her love for her pet was not matched by her desire to do all the dirty work that goes with it. Nevertheless, the three of us all got along until one week it started to rain. And rain. And rain.

Nobody told me I was meant to put the guinea pig cage up on bricks. And I still don't know how strong guinea pigs are as swimmers. I'm guessing not very. I came home one day amidst torrential downpours to find poor Bubbles swimming against the tide in so many ways. Hattie's pride and joy was still with us though. Bedraggled but not quite drowned, flailing in the flooded cage in our flooded garden, Bubbles was hanging on in there. I did my best David Hasselhoff impression and went all *Baywatch* as I waded to the rescue. I plucked Bubbles out of the watery prison and returned to the house. Whilst all was well that night and for a few days more, it was clear the ordeal had all been too much for what is essentially a land-based mammal. Bubbles developed a really bad skin complaint and died a couple of weeks later. There was an emotional burial in the garden, with father and daughter clinging tightly to each other as she suffered her life's first significant loss.

Eight years later we were idly chatting about dear old Bubbles. I was talking about the emotional moment we'd shared but Hattie kept referring to how nice her granddad (my Old Man) had been around that time. He wasn't in the garden with us that day so I asked Hattie what she meant. She wasn't talking about our mini funeral, she was reflecting on the wonder of once owning one of those amazing winter-coat altering guinea pigs she had not seen before or since! She told me, 'I realised pretty soon after getting the guinea pig home that this wasn't Bubbles. Bubbles was a girl and ours was a boy!' The complete aesthetic overhaul she was prepared to believe in but the fact our imposter now sported a penis she most certainly was not. Rumbled!

I first went through all of that with Hattie well over ten years ago but the trial of welcoming more pets into our home surely beckons anew. Alice, my six-year-old, wants a guinea pig now whilst Ava, who would probably be perfectly at ease rolling about in a basket with a slavering, slobbering Doberman, has just started pestering me for a pony. Heaven help us all!

28

Do I Hate Trisha?

'If the wind changes direction, your face will stay that way';
'If you don't behave you're grounded'; 'If you're naughty
again I'll take you on *The Jeremy Kyle Show*'! These are just
a few of the threats handed out by those looking to keep
their kids on the straight and narrow. When I was a kid, most
of my mates were prompted towards better behaviour with
semi-scary stories about The Bogeyman, The Monster in the
Wardrobe or some other figure who would come out of the
woodwork if we didn't do as we were told.

I thought most tall tales of that type would always remain
in childhood but when I first joined ITV, I was given another
cautionary tale about a monster that could prowl the corridors and dressing rooms I was soon to take over. Just as when
I was a boy, this tale was told in order to save me from myself.
It was part of a message sent loud and clear that things in
my life were about to change and that I was not to abuse any
newfound power and influence that came my way. Their talk
was basically a stylised variation of that old showbiz maxim
'be nice to everyone on the way up because you will meet
them on the way down,' but the monster they spoke of was
me – a sort of potential Ghost of Kyle Future!

Many grizzled TV veterans have bruises and war stories galore from promising 'talent' who let it all go to their head. So newcomers are warned about the dangers of getting too big for their boots at the very start of their TV careers. At least I was. It was a bit like an inoculation, a jab given to me as a TV toddler to spare me from the worst excesses that might follow in later life, if opportunity really did knock, and fame and fortune came trampling in after. When I signed on to present my show my polite advice to keep grounded was given added poignancy though: 'Jeremy,' they said, 'you must never do a Trisha!'

Five years ago I got a massive break when I auditioned at ITV to take over a show and a team that until very recently had been run by Trisha Goddard. Rumours abounded in the press that her defection to Channel 5 was the result of shabby treatment by her former bosses. It was not until I landed the job that I began to hear other, contrary tales, with some telling me that she had gone the way of all celebrities 'too big for their boots' and left having become too horribly difficult to deal with. I'll never know the truth of what happened but the warning I got every day after I signed, and for many a long month after, was never to 'do a Trisha'.

Now, I may be reporting this unfairly. As I point out all the time on my show, there are two sides to every story. I was only ever privy to the side of those Trisha left behind but there were just as many who ditched ITV to join her at Channel 5 so she clearly generated a lot of loyalty, too. On my new team the angst and acrimony that affected so many caught up in Trisha's departure undoubtedly left a bitter taste. Jobs and mortgages were threatened and those most exposed to this uncertainty were those at the bottom of the pile (isn't it always); the hard-working majority upon whose labours every TV star's success is built. In those circumstances you can understand why people who've worked slavishly to help a show triumph might feel aggrieved or even betrayed by a presenter's choice to move on. In fact it is not uncommon in such situations for once-loyal ex-colleagues to rise up and tell anyone around what a monster their previous presenter had turned in to. They will juxtapose tales of the meek, mild-mannered know-nothing who came into TV full of gratitude, grace and courtesy with those of the rude and bullying tyrant they morphed into. Invariably, 'it all started going wrong when fame went to their head, when they started believing their own hype.'

I have never met Trisha and can only recall ever seeing her twice. Both times, quite freakily, I was at the Pride of Britain awards, walking down the red carpet and posing for pictures. Each time, a year apart, I looked behind to see Trisha, ten yards behind, doing the same for the massed ranks of photographers. When my show started to do well in the ratings, a story seemed to build that there was some sort of bad blood between me and her. Headlines like 'Trisha Trashed' in the *Sun*, as my show started to regularly pull in one million more viewers than hers probably didn't help, but for my part, I have never had a problem with her. Although I admit my view of her might have been coloured by the reports I heard from those she left behind.

The point was, Trisha had moved on (for whatever reason) and I was grateful to get the chance to be her replacement. I met my new office, listened intently to their stories and made a vow to not do whatever it is they were accusing my predecessor of whilst also doing my very best to make *our* show even better than hers had been. It later transpired that my new show was to go up against Trisha's at 9.25 each morning – the battle lines had been drawn. For some. My office, I could tell, were desperate to beat theirs. This was a point of personal pride for them, but I was just focused on taking it all in, keeping my head above water and doing the best I could. She had her show, I had mine and I was just looking forward to getting on with my life.

A year or so down the line, people started claiming how Trisha was beginning to badmouth me in the press. I don't know – was she feeling the pressure of falling behind in the ratings or trying to drum up some publicity for her new show? Whatever the reason, she had apparently started to target me in interviews. I believe she said that I was a bully, she would be scared to be stuck in a lift with me and that she couldn't bear my brand of 'shouty-shouty' shows.

I found this a little disingenuous, if I am honest. Our shows, although different, were founded on the same sorts of principles and both allow guests to become heated when talking through their issues. I found it a bit odd that she would take such personal offence at the success I was having with the team she had apparently dumped for more money elsewhere. She said in one interview that 'you could put a dancing monkey' on at 9.25 a.m. on ITV1 and it would do well when the truth is the programme we took over from long-term, *People's Court,* had flatly failed.

Maybe she was being deliberately provocative. Maybe she was feeling the pressure now that she was making her own show with her own company and it wasn't delivering the ratings she had hoped or promised. Maybe she genuinely doesn't like me, even though she has never spoken to me. I don't know. However, one thing I am sure of is that I increasingly have a lot of respect for her. I have empathy for the situation she found herself in at ITV and genuine sympathy for how things turned out for her at Channel 5.

I am five years into my job at ITV and I have seen how easy it is to become frustrated with certain people or processes. I am no longer the new boy and yet still some people insist on talking to me as if I were a wet-behind-the-ears newcomer from a foreign land. I wonder at some of the decisions that sometimes get made around me and see the looks on people's faces if I dare to speak my mind or, God forbid, give an opinion! And I know full well that if I upped and left tomorrow, many of those who are so nice to me in the studios today would be the first in the queue to slag me off to my replacement tomorrow.

I honestly do get where Trisha must have been coming from and I have now experienced many of the frustrations that, after seven years doing the same show, must have become too much for her. I bear her no ill will and if she came up to me at the next Pride of Britain awards I'd be the first to shake her hand and invite her to have a drink. I'm sure we've got more in common than we think and a fair truckload of swappable stories to share about the job we both do. More than that, I genuinely admire her.

The one thing I really respect in my peers in this industry is longevity. To build and maintain a lasting career in this business requires talent and sound judgement combined with hard work, of course. Trisha has been in television far longer than I have so I can only applaud her for making the best of it and sticking around as long as she has. She has shown real ambition to make the most of her talents, in a way that I hope I can learn from, emulate and one day better. I don't know why she left ITV but I do know she struck out on her own, took a chance on herself and made the best of it. She gave it a go and that takes guts. Yes, she was shunted around the ratings so we didn't go head-to-head and yes I know she finally succumbed, winding down production of her Channel 5 show as the Credit Crunch took its toll. But she felt forced into a gamble and, with back to the wall, made it work for the most part. Fair play.

I've followed in her footsteps so far. I started a show just like she did, when she took over from Vanessa Feltz. I have helped build it to heights I didn't dare dream of when I began five years ago and now I'm excited about all the future holds. But I know that could all change at the drop of a hat. It could all come crashing down around my ears tomorrow, I could be shunted out the door and the team I love now might then be the ones to usher in my replacement with a cautionary tale of how they must 'never do a Jeremy!'

29

First Night Nerves

Some of the very first *Jeremy Kyle Shows* ever recorded were done with a certain Mr Jerry Springer watching from the wings! Before we launched my show, Jerry had flown over to film a month's worth of his own UK talk shows. They aired in the same ITV time slot, presumably to give viewers a similar fix to the one they had been used to with Trisha, and the one they would soon be getting with me. Now, hosting your own television show for the very first time is nerve-wracking enough, but doing it with the world famous king of the same format studying you from the sidelines is enough to induce a heart attack.

Having taken so long to get the job, I did not have much time to prove myself. An initial thirty-episode contract may seem like a substantial one but for a show like mine that works out to just a six-week run. ITV would therefore probably make their decision on whether or not this was working out within the first fortnight or so. That to me felt like pressure. Good pressure, exciting pressure – yes – but the sort of pressure that tells every part of your soul that you dare not mess this up. If you had asked me beforehand if this rookie wanted one of the most famous names on the planet to watch him as he tried to put his own stamp on a job that The Master had done with consummate brilliance for nearly twenty years, the answer would have been a tight, terse NO! However, he was there and the music had started; it was time to give it a go.

I might have felt a little better about things if I didn't have such a chequered past in this field – I am bad at making first professional impressions. My first ever gigs on the radio, my first ever radio roadshow – none of these went well, and certainly not according to plan . . .

When I started on radio, all I had to do to was say my name, tell the listeners the name of the song and then hit 'play'. I'd had a week to prepare, what could be easier? OK, it didn't help that I'd spent the week hyperventilating about what was to be my debut as the host of a radio show called the *Overnight Express*, recorded in Bristol, for the GWR network. I was to be let loose on the controls for four hours from 2 a.m. one Sunday morning. Slight problem though, nobody had told me the first thing about how to operate the equipment. Everyone had disappeared for the weekend and I was just left to get on with it. Thankfully a lovely man called James Richards stayed behind that night to help me operate the machinery that was totally alien to me. Unfortunately his help was not nearly enough to save us.

Wheezing with nerves like I'd just sprinted up fifteen flights of stairs, I looked at the microphone in front of me and waited for my cue. The light came on, my chest tightened and in between hurried gulps of breath I gave an introduction that sounded like it was being dragged out of me on a waterboard at Guantanamo Bay.

'He-llo (wheeze). I'm (gasp). Jeremy (wheeze). Kyle (gasp).

And (wheeze). This (gasp). Is. Over. Night. Ex. Press. Here's. Ti-na. Tur-ner. With. Sim-ply. The. Best. Which. I'm. Not. Sorry.'

With the world's worst opening to a radio show now murdered, all I had to do was play the music. It was a blessed relief to hear Tina's band strike up on the CD player. I started to breathe again and went over to load up the next song . . . *Silence.* The music had stopped. Everything had gone quiet. I looked around for answers and saw to my horror that the silence was down to me. Far from sorting the next CD, I'd actually hit 'eject' on the one we were playing!

Oh dear. Panic, sweat and now the cardinal sin of radio – dead air. I attempted a recovery and stuttered through the next half hour or so before throwing everything over to the phones, hoping some interesting callers might save us. I needn't have bothered. For the first time in the station's history there was nobody phoning in, not even a wrong number. They had probably all given up after the first few seconds. I would have! Throughout the whole four hours, I got only one call. It was from a farmer and his wife in Newbury who were staying up all night to nurse one of their cows through a birth! They remained on the line for most of the night and just before we signed off their cow delivered an eighty-seven pound calf they said they were going to call Jezza!

Only those tuning in to morbidly witness the radio-presenting equivalent of a live on-air car crash would have stayed listening that night. Thankfully the man who was to become my mentor and next boss was too (the legend that was Mr Phil Easton), and he decided that there was something in me that was worth taking a chance on. He hired me for a stint on Orchard FM. I was to have a ball at this station, but not before my own propensity for putting my foot in it from the off had reared its head again. This time though, it had at least waited until my third attempt at presenting a weekend breakfast show.

Roughly two hundred thousand people tuned in to listen to me that sunny morning in Somerset. I was sat in the lovely house near the M5 where Orchard was stationed, getting ready to go on air. The studio overlooked the beautiful countryside and there was a massive bay window across the other side of the room where everyone went to have a quick fag break between songs. This being such a wonderful summery morning, I thought I'd do the same. Chirpily, I launched into the intro I hoped would buy me some time for a quick smoke.

'Good morning, it's great to be here and I hope you're having a lovely Sunday morning wherever you are. It's ten past eight and I'm about to play you three songs in a row while I go for a chuff!'

Nothing like honesty, I thought. It really was that nice a day, I figured people would understand. Sadly my boss didn't. The smoking he could handle, my turn of phrase he could not. I was not a local lad so clearly I wasn't well versed in the local vernacular. 'Chuff' he explained to me, meant something very different to 'smoke' down in these parts. 'Chuff', he not-so-delicately went on, was the name most of Orchard's listeners would give to a lady's naughty parts! Oops, I think I'd just told half the county that I was popping over to that window for some sort of 'roll in the bay!'

Within days of working at another station, Invicta Radio

in Kent, I made the mistake of mentioning during one of my first shows that I felt hungry. For about the next three months, pizzas were delivered endlessly to the studio and I was forever fending off the owners of a million and one fast food joints. They were convinced I was ordering food I had no intention of paying for as some sort of prank. IT WASN'T ME! I'd been stitched up by a listener. It felt like I had to take my life in my hands whenever I left the studio and God help me if ever I *did* actually fancy ordering a takeaway pizza!

By the time I made it to BRMB in Birmingham I could at least summon the required composure to speak and breathe normally. I was careful not to mention fast food, fag breaks or anything that could be misconstrued as sordid, sexual funny business. I'd also learned by then that if ever I needed a toilet break all I had to do was put on 'Hotel California' and hope I could do whatever needed to be done in less than six and half minutes! I was confident by this point because I was comfortable in what I was doing. However, it only took the introduction of one new role, responsibility, job or face for me to regress to the panicked kid from the *Overnight Express* who kept getting it wrong. Three months into my BRMB career and my nerves were shredded all over again, this time courtesy of the Spice Girls.

I was dispatched to London on BRMB's behalf to conduct a brief press interview with the Spice Girls as part of their promotional work for their movie, *Spiceworld*. Every network radio station in Britain had, it seemed, sent the jewel in their crown to dazzle both the Girls and their listeners. As a result there were about forty breakfast show hosts and their producers all preparing busily in the lobby, and then there was me. People were scribbling furiously in a way that left me a little uneasy. What were they doing? It transpired that they were all trying to concoct a series of perfect questions that would skewer the ten minutes each of us was allowed in the Spice bubble in just the way their listeners demanded. I was sat there reading a copy of the *Sun* feeling a little out of my depth, woefully underprepared and clearly not quite getting what it took to make the most of my stab at an 'exclusive' celebrity interview.

As it happened, I was also first up. I walked in and saw two Spice Girls busily filing their Spice Nails, one was absent-mindedly fiddling with her Spice Hair and the other two were just enjoying a little Spice Chat. I took my seat and looked through the window into the studio next door, waiting for my cue. As I did, I saw the cream of the commercial radio crop staring back at me. Dr Fox, Chris Tarrant and Steve Penk were all very big names in radio at that time and seeing them reduced me to a quiver. Oh, this really was a big deal! Instantly I wished I'd filled the blank pad in front of me with reams of notes and incisive questions. As it was I knew nothing and was therefore a tad exposed to say the least. All I knew about the Spice Girls' film was that it featured a load of cameos from established stars. Meat Loaf played their tour bus driver, for example, but I also remembered that Michael Barrymore had been given the role of some Sergeant Major figure who had to teach the Girls how to march or something like that. It wasn't much to go on but with the Capital radio gods looking on I knew it was time to dive in. It was now or never.

'So, Baby, what was it like being drilled by Michael Barrymore then?'

I wasn't being funny at all, and certainly wasn't trying to be. But as I looked up I saw all my betters in the studio next door fall about laughing. Poor 'Baby Spice' Emma Bunton probably didn't know if I was dropping deliberate double entendres, being really rude or coming on to her like some sleazeball in a strip bar. The presenters next door didn't care, they were pointing and laughing and lapping up my misery.

Thankfully it was short-lived. Word had got out that the Spice Girls were in the studio and half the nation's teenagers were starting to converge on Leicester Square. The Spice Bouncers and Spice Management team, under orders from the police no less, came in to bundle them out of a back door before there was any hormonal stampede by the gathering outside to force their way in. Of all the presenters there for interviews that day, I was the only one who got to ask the Spice Girls a question. And what a question. But it was all they had and everyone around the country had to use it and as much of the answer to it as any of the girls could muster, before Security had barged in to cut the whole thing short!

I was no better on the road. My very first radio roadshow again took place down in Somerset. There were about a thousand people partying in front of this stage and it was my job to keep them 'up' and to get them going between songs, before whoever was presenting came back on air. During one extended break it fell to me to give out some free prizes to some 'lucky winners' I was to pluck from the audience and then enjoy a bit of on-stage banter with. I saw one particular lady who looked like she'd be loud and so I helped her up on to the stage. She wasn't nearly as animated as I'd hoped she would be and so, with nerves rising once more, I tried to fill time with her in a way that kept everyone else interested. Trying to keep things just the right side of saucy, I announced to the whole crowd that this big blotchy mark on her neck must be proof that she'd been getting up to no good in the crowd. Who was the lucky devil who'd been giving her love bites in the front row, I demanded to know! The crowd was laughing and I think I may even have called the poor woman 'a dirty mare' as I screamed at everyone to stare at the evidence on her neck. They were with me, they wanted it revealed who'd given her the love bite so I thrust my microphone under her chin and demanded she tell all. She looked back at me, crushed. Crestfallen, she announced to the world that the blemish I'd belittled so bullishly was in fact a birthmark. And one she'd had a complex about for years! At times like that I have to reflect that it would probably have been better if the nerves plaguing me beforehand had done a proper job and killed me!

Inside work or out, I am just the same when meeting new people. One of my very best friends is a total diamond who I first met about three years ago. I was introduced to him at a party, a menacing man mountain by the name of Martin and I thought he must be the local hard nut. Proper Eastender, gruff voice, shaved head and arms the size of both my legs put together – it is safe to say I seem to shrink a little whenever I stand next to him. I would trust this man with my kids' lives, no questions asked, but back then I thought he looked a bit dodgy. Anyway, as we got chatting I noticed a big scar running down his neck. Probably from a fight or some nightclub glassing, I thought. We continued talking but in the end, curiosity got the better of me, as it tends to do.

I had to ask. Trying to play it cool and supposing he was used to balls-out chats about fighting and stabbing, I went all Del Boy and casually leaned in to point at his throat. 'So, how d'ya get that, knife was it?' Not one to suffer fools, Martin's reply was simple, effective and truthful in a way that made my toes curl with embarrassment. 'Cancer, you c*nt!' was all he said.

These are but a few of the terrible tales I could tell to explain how first night nerves have sometimes sabotaged my best intentions. And so it was with some trepidation that I took to the stage for my first few *Jeremy Kyle Shows*. I was waiting for something, anything, *everything* to go wrong. And to have it all blow up with Jerry Springer watching would have been just typical.

A few of those early shows were a bit bizarre, beset as they were by the sorts of teething troubles that all productions endure in their infancy. For me, dressing like an ice cream salesman felt a bit weird but I didn't dare say anything about my dreaded stripey jackets. For all of us, audiences were another problem. Nobody knew me or my name and so a ticket offering a free seat at the all new *Jeremy Kyle Show* was anything but hot. Our producers were literally in the streets bribing old ladies and pressganging passers-by into the studio for a little watch of something new. The gaps they couldn't fill with their silver tongues they filled with their own backsides. Most of my first ten or twenty shows felt a bit like Groundhog Day as every time I looked around, the same faces from the office were staring down at me from the audience. And it was a good job too, on one day in particular.

Back then, right at the start, I didn't know that we could

stop filming any time. Of course I know we can now, and we regularly do, to fix sound problems, lights and change tapes. However, until I learned all this I always just carried on listening and gabbing and trying to sort things out as we went. During one show I was chatting away merrily, sat on my little step. As I got up my microphone battery pack unclipped itself from the back of my trousers. I could feel it swinging behind me like a big swishing tail – I thought the whole production was in jeopardy if I didn't rescue the situation. Out of the corner of my eye, I spied one of my producers a few rows up in the audience. I backed towards him trying not to trip over the swinging mic pack as I went. Once in front of him I gestured at him to help me tidy myself up, trying not to give the game away to my guests, the audience or the watching director in the gallery. Of course the guys in the gallery could see everything and they just wondered why I was continuing with the show whilst looking so cagey.

Worse was to come. The producer I had asked to help readjust me scooped up the dangling pack and set about re-lodging it in the back of my waistband. He couldn't get any purchase though and the director, who just for her own curiosity's sake had had one of her cameramen zoom in on us both to see what we were doing, later said the scene looked like I was being aggressively molested from behind by an audience member. Worse for me, I think Jerry Springer was watching all this unfold. Perfect, I try and show I can be trusted to control this brand new show and there I am, being fisted by the first audience member I stop in front of! Just bloody marvellous!

Thankfully the initial hitches ended there. A few hiccups

have happened from time to time since but nothing we haven't so far been able to handle. I guess the main thing I lacked then was experience and without it the old confidence can sometimes feel a bit brittle.

As you can see, 'first night nerves' have been at the root of a few embarrassing cock-ups to date so it was especially nice to get some sound advice from Mr Springer on how I might beat them in future. The specific pearls of wisdom won't seem much to anyone reading now. 'Be yourself', 'Do it your way,', and 'good luck' could be described as fairly obvious, run-of-the-mill advice anyone could give. To me though it was everything. It wasn't so much the words, more the time he took to say them. He didn't need to be there but he chose to be and his presence actually turned out be a great help to me at that time. Essentially I was the man who was taking his job on UK screens and yet whenever he was about he let me know he was on hand for advice if I needed it. There was no looking over his shoulder, no pulling rank and none of the jealousy that would infect quite a few in the industry if they were in his position at that time. After one show we spent about an hour and half just chatting and he specifically told me that if I ever needed any help, all I had to do was call. To me that shows the measure of Jerry Springer and that is why I still hold him in such high regard today.

I never did make that call however, I got my head down and just got used to my show instead. Who knows though, with America looming, now might be the right time to pick up the phone. I wonder if he'd be so generous with his time and advice if I were requesting it in his own back yard? I guess we'll soon see.

30

A Military, Cross!

Did you know that more British personnel died from committing suicide *after* the Falklands War than were killed during the conflict itself? For a country that prides itself on never leaving fallen brethren behind in battle, I think it's a national disgrace that so many of our soldiers are seemingly left to rot the second they are discharged from military service.

I would implore anyone unmoved by that shocking statistic to attend an event like the Millies to see just how shameful and scandalous it really is. I went to the *Sun*'s Annual Military Awards ceremony in 2009 and left with a new appreciation of the debt we owe all those who fight so courageously on our behalf. They lay their lives on the line every day so that we never have to. They spill *their* blood in order to preserve *our* freedoms and yet thousands of them have their plight ignored by the society they fought so hard to protect, the second they are returned home. How can it be that so many of the brave souls who give everything for Queen and country get nothing from the rest of us at exactly the times when they need our help most?

It is bad enough that we send these people into war zones dangerously ill-equipped. I honestly don't know how some officials sleep at night knowing that they have deliberately denied our forces some of the kit they need. You'd think protecting soldiers' lives would be the priority – and it most certainly should be – but some of the resource shortages I have read about compromise our soldiers' ability to even *start* the missions they've been sent half way around the world to complete!

In the past couple of years we've had reports of not enough helicopters and not enough armoured vehicles. Worse, some of the ones we *do* have are out of commission or just not fit for purpose. We've had troops buying their own binoculars whilst watching their MoD supplied boots melt in the desert heat. We've had not enough machine guns, sub-standard ones that keep jamming, not enough night vision goggles, insufficient body armour and the frankly embarrassing admission that some of our soldiers have felt forced to scrounge extra kit off of our allies. Our troops are dubbed 'The Borrowers' by their American counterparts such is the scale of their kit lending to us but I also read that some of our soldiers have been forced to go cap in hand to our Estonian allies – Europe's smallest army! Lives are being risked that shouldn't be. Some are being lost that needn't be and that is both an insult and a tragedy.

I was driving to Manchester through the snow that swamped us at the start of 2010. I was on my way for filming but stopped as I sometimes do at Warwick Services to grab a bite and stretch the legs. There, right outside KFC, I met two squaddies in between tours of Afghanistan. We got talking and when I came to leave I wished them well and thanked them for all they were doing in the service of this country. One of them turned back and said, 'Do you know what, that's all any of us want to hear.' He went on to explain how upset he and his colleagues had sometimes felt, back home of all places, because of an apparent lack of support for the war. He made it quite clear that the war was not his choice, but fighting in it was his job. He hadn't asked to go to Afghanistan just as none of his brothers-in-arms had begged to go to Iraq. They just followed orders, orders that carry a high enough price already, without the added tax of abuse and ill feeling people simply don't deserve back home.

Back at the Millies and I was treated to one of the most awe-inspiring nights of my life. I thought I had seen all the world could offer in terms of courage and bravery when I attended the Pride of Britain awards but this was right up there, too.

The fact is, after filming some *Jeremy Kyle Shows* I can get a bit down. Some stories just get to me and I can be left with a frustration that occasionally makes me despair for some of the lives people lead in this country. I may have been feeling a little like this when I turned up at the Millies because the turnaround in emotions in me by the end of the evening was truly astounding. I left there wishing we could just bottle the spirit and the teamwork and the togetherness that was on display in everyone I met. If I could, I'd stash it on the shelves of our TV studio and splash it on some of those guests whose selfishness and laziness is at the root of their problems. It really was magical to behold.

We were there to recognise some truly outstanding feats of gallantry and I sat open-mouthed, endlessly clapping like a sea lion at feeding time as the awards were given out. I heard how an ex-cabbie from Birmingham (Able Seaman Edmond Grandison) only joined the Navy part time to help out but ended up keeping the seas safe from Somali pirates, fighting off attackers from two vessels with bravery that stunned his colleagues. Another Able Seaman, Kate Nesbit, a medic, ran seventy yards through enemy fire to treat a wounded soldier on a battlefield in Helmand Province in Afghanistan. She was there for forty-five minutes. Under fire, she risked her own life to save his, just like Corporal Carl Thomas, a man who saved *thirty-five* lives administering treatment to fallen comrades in the most bombed outpost in Afghanistan! I could list every one of the amazing people I saw that night but I couldn't do them all the justice they deserve. Look them up yourself via the Millies on the *Sun*'s website, read what they went through and then try, really try to imagine what that must have been like for them. After that, just sit back in wonder as I did. And then when you've got over all that, please look up these next two names.

So taken was I with all the astonishing stories being told in front of me that at first I didn't even notice the people who were actually sat right alongside me that night. Something should have stirred in me sooner, as everyone in the room seemed to be heading for our table. Soldiers and top brass alike kept flocking to a man I later learned was none other than Lance Corporal Johnson Gideon Beharry. His name might not be immediately recognisable to you but his stirring acts of courage should be. We were at a ceremony celebrating military bravery but it seemed that all the military in attendance – even the winners and regardless of rank – were all coming over to bow down to this one man. And here's why.

Johnson Beharry was serving in Iraq in 2004. He was just twenty-five at the time and he was called to drive his Warrior armoured vehicle to help a foot patrol caught up in a horrible ambush. The Warrior was hit on all sides by rocket-propelled grenades, causing untold damage to the vehicle and downing radio communications. Private (as he was at the time) Beharry's platoon commander, the vehicle's gunner and a number of other soldiers were injured. The only way to steer the vehicle home and out of harm's way was for him to open the hatch and expose his head to gunfire that was shredding him from every angle. His cabin was filled with flames and noxious smoke and while he was driving, his helmet was pierced by gunfire. No matter, he drove his crippled Warrior through the ambush undeterred, leading five other vehicles towards safety as he did so.

He got the stricken convoy as far as he could but the rest of the journey would have to be on foot. He wasn't interested in being the only one saved that day but everyone around him was badly wounded and they couldn't get anywhere without him. Realising this, Private Beharry slung his commander over his shoulder and walked him to another waiting Warrior out of the line of fire. He returned to do the same for the vehicle's gunner before then going back a *third* time to guide the rest of his disoriented walking wounded to safety too. He was under fire throughout and eventually collapsed with exhaustion, but not until he had ushered the last of his crew to safety. Unsurprisingly, he got cited for 'valour of the highest order' that day but, believe it or not, his best was still to come.

About six weeks later, Private Beharry was out in another Warrior when he and his crew came under heavy rocket-propelled grenade fire once more. One of the grenades detonated six inches from his head, causing him horrendous injuries as it exploded in his face. More rockets hit, injuring his commander and many of the crew inside, just as before. With blood pouring into his eyes and his head virtually in pieces, this man somehow managed to retain control of the vehicle and back it out to safety in the dead of night with next to no visibility. He moved the Warrior out of the enemy's 'kill zone' and as a result enabled all of his crew to be extracted and taken back to safety once more. The minute his job was done, his crew safe, he lost consciousness.

Johnson Beharry drifted into a coma and suffered head injuries so severe that he has never been allowed to return to active duty. And do you know, that's the one thing he would probably most like to do – get right back out there and keep helping the regiment he was so proud to serve.

He was awarded the Victoria Cross, the highest military decoration for valour in the British and Commonwealth armed forces. He is the youngest person ever to be awarded the VC and the first living person since 1969. Not only that, he's the best looking man I've ever seen! Head half blown to bits and put back together with titanium plates, you'd be forgiven for thinking I would be talking to some Robosoldier cyborg, but this guy looked like he'd just stepped off the catwalk in Milan – he was gorgeous!

Unfortunately he can't link up with his old regiment and now has a desk job with the army. However, he spends a lot of his time talking up what needs to be done to properly support the servicemen and women of this country – both in war and back home. Selfless to the last, and in that respect, he is a lot like the other amazing person sat near me that night. Her name is Christina Schmid.

You may remember her as the wife of a fallen army bomb

disposal expert, Olaf Schmid. He was killed on his final scheduled day in the field in Afghanistan. This is the woman who wowed the nation with her articulacy and dignity in the face of overwhelming grief, when her husband's body was repatriated to this country. Carrying out her husband's wishes to highlight what still needs to be done to protect our troops in Afghanistan and, indeed, look after them when they return home, she somehow refused to buckle beneath the pain of her monumental loss. She would have been entitled to dissolve into tears at any point but instead she talked of the need for everyone in this country to properly respect the work our Armed Forces do each day. She rightly wanted to ensure that the government stepped up to properly look after each and every person serving – both in terms of kit on the ground and help when they get home. She wanted no one to take for granted the sacrifices being made for us and never to treat horrific but preventable injuries as 'business-as-usual'.

I found her, and everything she said over the weeks around her husband's untimely death truly amazing, but it wasn't until I spoke to her that I got a proper sense of what she was going through. In amongst the grief, the loss, the looking after her five-year-old son and trying to do right by her husband's last wishes; in amongst the public speaking, the private turmoil and all the media attention being thrust upon her was another devastating piece of news. Twenty-four hours before her husband's body was flown home, she was made redundant. That just made her stoicism all the more admirable to me. I would have crumbled long before.

It would be easy to go to an event like the Millies and leave on a high, having only basked in the celebratory aspect of everything that is rightly acknowledged on such a night.

That, though, would be to ignore the hopes and wishes of the people that really matter – the soldiers themselves. None of those receiving awards wanted any limelight they could not share with their regiments. The back slapping was all well and good but the overriding message coming from everyone I met was, 'support us'. Not just morally, but practically. And make no mistake, that support is needed because too many of our soldiers – and their families – are being spat, broken, back onto Civvy Street, left to go it alone, abandoned in the most appalling way. If people like Johnson Beharry and Christina Schmid can put all their own emotions to one side to push that message, given all they have gone through, it is the least I can do.

Twenty-four thousand people have left the British Armed Forces in recent years and a steadily rising number seem to have been discarded without anything or anyone to assist their ongoing adjustment to civilian life. Depression, stress and an inability to cope are in evidence everywhere and so, tragically, is a lack of basic support. Even those who have heroically survived the most horrific of injuries are seeing the fabric of their life crumble once they have been ushered out of rehab. They are being too quickly pushed back into the pressures of everyday life and for too many, they are too much to bear.

The camaraderie and support that saw them through the toughest of times in war can be pulled from under them in an instant, leaving them horribly exposed. That is just not fair. These people don't ask for millions even though they probably deserve them. They don't really ask for anything and they shouldn't bloody well have to. No government should need to be prodded to properly help the people who have spilled blood for them. Basic loyalty should dictate that we provide every assistance to soldiers who have lost limbs. Duty should compel us to support the families torn apart by the bereavements brought to their door by our wars. Ex-servicemen and women should never need to ask for help – it should be given. They should be waving it away by virtue of having too much, not paying for it themselves as those funding their own rehab now have to. But it is not just rehabilitation, re-integration is just as big a problem.

Some statistics I've read state that one in ten of our country's prison population is a Forces veteran. There are apparently 12,000 on parole and 8,500 actually in prison – that's only slightly less than the total amount of serving British troops in Afghanistan! I don't say this to have a go at them. I point it out because it surely highlights the need to give our troops more help than they are getting to adjust to civilian life.

Apparently, one in ten homeless people on British streets is ex-Services personnel. Post Traumatic Stress Disorder is rife, as are mental health problems. Alcohol and drug abuse is particularly prevalent. Joblessness is soaring and many who leave the Forces have complained that they have not been equipped with any of the skills needed to function in 'normal' society. This puts pressures on families and partially explains why marriages among ex-Forces families are disintegrating at an alarming rate.

I know there is a lot of excellent work being done out there by a whole range of charities. Organisations like Help for Heroes are plugging the funding gaps and providing support. There are many other groups like them, supported by millions of us up and down the country and I'll only ever commend the great work they do. My problem is a case of, where would we be without them? The statistics are horrifying and if the benevolence and generosity of the public was taken away where would our brave boys and girls be then? What 'help for heroes' would really be on offer to all those disfigured, disabled or in any way disadvantaged by signing up to fight for this country?

Nobody likes to feel used in life but too many in our Armed Forces clearly have been. I've always steadfastly supported every man and woman who serves this country in our military. I've always thought we should do everything we could to stand by them, and until now I rather thought we were. Clearly I was wrong. I really am left scratching my head as to how those good people and that great spirit I encountered at the Millies would ever be left to go to waste. But the stats suggest it might just happen. Those towering examples of hard work, dedication and humanity may be tossed aside in a few years' time and none of us would ever know. This cannot be allowed to happen. Ever. Great Britain must never turn her back on anyone who risks their life to fight under this nation's flag!

31

Room Service(s)

What do you do in a hotel that you wouldn't do anywhere else? How does the excitement of breezing through a huge revolving door, clip-clopping across the grand marble reception and being ushered into an expensive suite corrupt you? It can't help but have an effect on most people and I have seen with my own eyes just how often it does! If you think you are immune, imagine how it would feel to have worked 'below stairs' all your life before one day being allowed to run wild in the house above, while the Lord and Lady are away, and you'll not be far wrong. And it is the power and privilege that comes with this temporary shift in status that is too much for some of us to handle.

In a good hotel the concierge attends to your every whim, reception caters for all your needs. Your bags are ferried by personal porters and food is delivered to your very bed if you so desire. Make one call and something will be delivered a-sizzling on a silver salver, click your fingers and things get cleaned and pressed into pristine condition. Toilet rolls are folded into arrows to make the tiresome business of tearing off a piece that bit easier to bear(!), chocolates get left on your pillow each night. A Turn Down team even pulls back a corner of the covers of your newly made bed each evening, just to make your own personal journey aboard the snugglebus to Bedfordshire that bit less stressful. Amidst such unrestrained opulence some of us can become mini kings with no thought for the courts we now command. We feel entitled to behave in a way we know is not right but that somehow seems acceptable at the time. Our normal codes of conduct get checked in at the door along with the luggage. It has happened to us all – so, come on, be honest – what did *you* do that you shouldn't when you last checked in to a posh hotel?

Some people steal the toiletries. I know of at least two friends with an almost pathological propensity for taking every shampoo or shower gel they can from any hotel room they visit. One will call down to get them re-stocked three times a day! He thinks that they think he's just a very hygienic man, but come off it, nobody believes he's bathing six times a day – everyone can see he's just filling his bag with some nice miniature smellies for when he gets home. Most people have done that I'd imagine, dragging out life in their little lap of luxury for just a few showers more once they've returned home. And we've probably all harrumphed defensively when questioned . . . 'I've paid for them, I'm having them!'

Others I know have tried to squeeze the 'free' slippers or even the towels and dressing gowns into their bags for use back home! I have never been down this road and as I have had to point out on numerous occasions, such things are not free. They are no more gifts than the TV at the end of the bed but some people just don't get it. If they are checked in for a two night stay they almost see it as some sort of challenge to claw back the room charge with as many 'free-bies' as they can. I've heard of people topping up with water half-necked drinks from the mini-bar not to mention a whole variety of excuses to try and get that coveted upgrade to a more luxurious room.

I will confess I have had my moments. I have been known to get a touch too light-fingered at the 'help-yourself-to-as-much-as-you-like' buffet. At least that's what I think it was called. 'Eat all you like' I actually translated to 'take all you can'. Fed up with being stung for forty quid every time one of my kids wanted a lunchtime nibble after barely touching their breakfast, I thought I'd get ahead of the game by smuggling a few muffins and bananas out of the early morning dining room. Wrapping them up in napkins and hiding them in the bottom of the buggy, I must have looked like some kind of Fagin. I lacked grace, dignity and was very probably wrong but I wasn't going to get stung again. After a few dips in the pool, just an hour later, when the kids got hungry again and pestered for food, I could enjoy my sad moment of triumph. Waving away my wife's attempt to call over a waiter, I dug into the bottom of the buggy and unfurled the stolen snacks from their napkins. I might as well have been lifting the FA Cup at Wembley. I held my muffins aloft and presented them to my children with all the pride of a caveman bringing back his first ever kill!

I have seen a fair few things going on in hotels that have made me rub my eyes in disbelief. Hotels are a weird 'other world' where the normal rules and standards of life don't seem to apply. Decorum goes out the window with decent adults reduced to the level of willfully misbehaving children on double doses of sugar. Of course in these grown-ups' playgrounds the 'sugar' of choice is normally alcohol, and far too much of it. With no need to stay straight for a journey home, the holiday vibe kicks in and adults in hotels – whether there for work, play or anything else, resort to the sort of behaviour you might find in evidence at a particularly boozy office party.

My first encounter of this sort was one that still causes me to blush. ITV pay for me to stay in a lovely Manchester hotel for a couple of days each week, as that's where my show is filmed. I've moved between three wonderful hotels since 2005 and I won't embarrass any one of them by specifically naming where some of the following took place. Suffice to say I am still plenty embarrassed enough for all concerned.

It was a Thursday night like any other and I'd just finished filming another three episodes of *The Jeremy Kyle Show*. I'd returned to the hotel, freshened up a touch and dined as normal in the restaurant downstairs. Knackered after a fourteen-hour day, a full feed and two glasses of red that had started to make the eyelids sag, I heard the siren calls of my bed and set off back to my room. As I came out of the lift I was in a sleepy world of my own but soon got wrenched back to reality by the scene outside my door. Was it reality? It looked like something out of a porn film. Was I dreaming? No. Definitely not. At the end of the corridor, right outside the door to my room, were two drunk lovers going at it hammer and tongs!

What clothes they still had on told me they were staying in the hotel for business, what was going on outside my front door only screamed they were there for pleasure. Who knows, maybe one of their businesses was pleasure? All I know is that I couldn't get round or past them to get to my room and I didn't want to tap them on the shoulder and ask to squeeze by. All I could do was get back in the lift and keep going up and down until they had finished, not unlike the couple themselves!

I must have gone back to the restaurant about four times. I looked like a total idiot as I kept passing reception, doing shuttle runs to and from the lift. I didn't want to grass on the people upstairs but I didn't really want to get close enough to ask them to stop either. I kept making excuses about losing my keys downstairs before popping back up every five minutes to see if the passion-a-thon was over and I could finally get to bed. Each time I went back to check I would see them in different states. Trousers round ankles, faces pressed against the window at the end of the hall – I can only imagine what the people on the street below were making of it all! Thankfully it ended eventually and after about my tenth ride in the lift they were gone. All I could see was a moonlit hand-print on the window outside my room, and as I padded along the darkened corridor I tried not to consider what else they might have left outside my door.

I reckon there's something about hotels that plays with the nation's libido. If you believe some of the more colourful reports concerning England footballers, 'ball skills' are always being practised when away at hotels, and normally long after training has finished. 'Playing away' has clearly taken on a whole new meaning for some of them.

Footballers do seem to be getting themselves caught out in some pretty indefensible positions, but leaving the morality aside for one moment – what about the stupidity? What is it about 'down' time that gets a professional athlete so 'up', anatomically? It is the same with rock stars too. What is it about a hotel room that makes it seem such a suitable place for drink and drugs and wild 'sexcess'? What is it in the water at a hotel that brings out the seediness in so many a young musician? Once upon a wayback, rock stars used to regularly trash hotel rooms or even hurl television sets out of hotel windows! What is all that about? They'd never do it at home and certainly not at their mother's house!

At one of the hotels I stayed at in Manchester I had another full-frontal assault on my eyes, this time whilst minding my business out on the bar's balcony. I was with Graham from the show and we were both enjoying a cheeky cigarette when down on the canal towpath below us we saw two guys walk past holding hands. They looked up, whispered to each other and did a bit of pointing our way. They seemed nice enough. I waved back and thought nothing of it. Five minutes later I was back on the balcony to make some phone calls when I caught sight of this blurring movement out of the corner of my eye. I wasn't sure if someone was waving at me so I leant forward to see more clearly and started waving back. Wrong move! The two guys were just visible in the shadows beneath a bridge on the towpath and I focused on a sight that was becoming familiar in this hotel – trousers round ankles. And no one was waving at me. In fact, my intervention was obviously putting them off what they had gone there to do and what I thought was friendly waving was two men gesturing at me furiously to stop perving and get back inside the bar. I did that instant, but not before the man standing behind had disengaged and thrust his genitals in the air at me. He then raised his middle finger and screamed something I couldn't quite hear as I scrambled back inside! Oops.

It is not just sex that seems to be unleashed all around me whenever I stay in hotels. The change in people when they are in hotels covers every attitude and, indeed, bodily function. I remember once walking out of my room in the early morning to find that the whole corridor had been graffitied with what looked like a load of melted Mars bars. There was a pile of this 'chocolate' outside my door and I only just missed stepping in it. As I walked to the lift trying to make sense of the new decorations, the smell hit me and then I knew. I don't know if someone was targeting me specifically or just losing themselves as so many do in hotels. Who knows, they may have had tummy trouble at just the moment they realised they had forgotten their key. Whatever, they had left the place looking like a Pete Doherty crack den!

Whilst I have never lost complete control in a hotel, I have had my moments. To my eternal shame I once let my frustrations boil over and I took it out on a poor receptionist. Typically, she had the last laugh, as did most of the hotel.

I hadn't slept well. I'd had an early start and a very long day of filming. I'd got up to shower and the water wasn't working. I'd ordered a taxi and it didn't arrive. I was late in the morning and even later in the evening because things had overrun. I'd left for work at half seven, got back at half ten at night but now couldn't get a table to eat. I went up to shower but the water was still cut off. I was irritated and, I admit, way too narky when I went looking for answers in Reception. The day's frustrations boiled over and whilst I didn't shout I did have a mini-huff when I heard that they still didn't know when the water would be back and couldn't give me a time when I might be able to eat.

I turned on my heel and flounced off. Not seeing the 'pull' sign on the door I was approaching, I continued at a pace and careered straight into it. It was not so much a 'push' as a shoulder charge but the door resisted, and I clonked my head on the glass with a chime that sounded like Big Ben. The door butted me back on the floor and I must have looked like an upturned beetle as I struggled for basic motor functions through the rage and acute embarrassment. There was much stifled giggling, not least because I'd left a big patch of TV make-up on the door where I'd stormed into it with my head! No worries, lesson learned, apologies all round and back to Earth, Jez. Sorry.

Muffin wrangling and the odd moment of irritation when I think the hotel gods are against me aside, that is about it for my own excesses in hotels. Mind you, I have been on hand when Graham has had to administer CPR to a man who collapsed twice the same night, both times just as we were walking past him. That was spooky and only added weight to my theory that something bizarre always happens in hotels, whenever I am there!

Thankfully I am too busy, too old and too much in love to ever get bored enough to ever seek to 'score' like an amorous international footballer at a hotel. That is not to say I have not been without female company, though. In my early days staying up in Manchester for filming I met up with the same lovely woman night after night. Her name was Maggie Jones.

You will probably know her as Blanche, the blunt-speaking battleaxe from *Coronation Street* but to me Maggie was always the softly spoken friend who provided perfect company at the end of every week. We'd have a few drinks, we'd chat and if things had become too heated or stressful in studio, Maggie was always on hand to provide the antidote. I have seen a lot of strange things going on in hotels and a lot of them have made quite an impact – memorable for all the wrong reasons. However, I couldn't let a chapter on hotels pass without mentioning Maggie. She made the pull of staying away from my family more bearable and gave me many a happy memory of life in Manchester hotels – and this time only for the right reasons. May she rest in peace.

32

Nudge the Judge Towards the Jury

Every newspaper article that appears about me includes the line, 'a judge once blasted *The Jeremy Kyle Show* as being televised bear-baiting' or something similar. I have been branded and that line is a piece of baggage that will follow me for as long as I am written about.

It's true that District Judge Alan Berg did slam my show in those terms but to my knowledge he also admitted to only ever having watched it once. I am accused of many things by many viewers, based only on what they see of my show on screen. That is fine but it ignores the huge efforts that go on by whole armies of people off-camera to ensure that all we do is in line with the law, this country's broadcasting codes of conduct and tip-top for the guests we invite on.

When I work on talkSPORT radio, I am often asked what I think of this football team or that. If I've only watched them once, I will say so and not presume to pass judgement on their whole season until such time as I've done my research on them. In my case, I believe Judge Berg was swayed towards a certain point of view by the testimony of a clued-up young lawyer, pressing all the right buttons in defense of his client. He gave his verdict on how he felt my show was run, based on what he had been told, and not on the truth of a situation he could have confirmed in ten minutes with a short visit and a little research (his court is about 500 yards from our studios, and we were only too happy to show him around so he could see first-hand what we really do!).

I don't think I'm alone in wondering whether this country's judges are really up to the job we employ them for. It seems as if every day I read about violent thugs being let off for their crimes or given totally inadequate sentences. Is it the system that is letting us down or are too many of today's judges too old and out-of-touch with the real world? Their judgments are meant to improve and protect society, punishing those who break the law whilst compensating victims with at least the reassurance that good will trump evil in a court of law. Justice must be seen to be done but all too often it is the criminals who seem to profit from their day in the dock.

I mean, how can it be that a man convicted of raping a nine-year-old boy can walk free with three years probation while pensioners get thrown in jail for refusing to pay council tax? In this country, anti-terror legislation has been used to snoop on people suspected of using the wrong bins while at the same time violent thugs are basically being told that they can carry on as normal despite being convicted of the most appalling crimes.

The list is endless. Over the course of just one week I read about a woman who received a mere 120 hours community service for nearly blinding an innocent bystander at a bar by viciously ramming a pint glass into her face. Two other thugs were released from prison – after just one day – despite being convicted of breaking a man's jaw and leaving him with a £2,000 bill to repair his shattered teeth. They went on to brag about 'the shortest jail term ever' whilst their victim was left with a life sentence of looking over his shoulder, worrying if his attackers might be lurking behind him. Unsurprisingly he fears for the courts' capacity and willingness to protect him if they do attack him again. Quite apart from sending the wrong message to every criminally-minded lout out there, these miscarriages of justice tell every law-abiding potential victim of crime that the law is not on their side, the system does not care about them and that yobs who inflict pain, years of misery and distress can do so with relative impunity.

Every newspaper and even my own daily postbag is stuffed with the names of criminals the public want to see locked up, but time and again they get away with sentences that don't reflect the seriousness of their crimes. In too many cases the convicted never even see the inside of a cell. I could fill this whole book with woefully inadequate sentences that stem from either the law's failure to protect us or a judge's inability to do what common sense dictates is right. But what lies behind these galling inconsistencies in sentencing? What's the real reason people posing no threat to society are pursued through the courts while remorseless thugs likely to reoffend are allowed to get away with doing just that?

Apparently, our prison population has reached its limit. We've got 85,000 criminals doing time at Her Majesty's Pleasure – a record high. £2.3 billion has been set aside to build thirteen new jails and as far as I'm concerned, they can't come soon enough. As I said, I was moved to speak out after being shocked by hearing about several stories of soft sentencing in just one week. But a quick look on the internet reveals that even when the prison population was lower, and presumably there was more space, the issue of crooks being let off when they should have been behind bars was still burning bright in Great Britain. Trawl back through any newspaper's online archives and with gut-thudding regularity you will find a drip-drip of stories where one crook or another has been let off too lightly or worse, let off altogether. Some escape justice via legal loopholes but a great many seem to be given too much benefit of too little doubt by judges out of touch with public feeling.

As if soft sentencing in the first place wasn't bad enough, I've also recently read that about 200 prisoners have been freed 'by mistake' over the last five years. Some of those released were on attempted murder charges and had to be rounded up all over again! It's farcical and would almost be funny – if it wasn't true.

If I were in charge, I'd propose some radical changes to the way we approach justice for hardened criminals in this country. First off, I wouldn't leave judges in sole charge of sentencing. I'd make the process more even-handed and representative of public opinion by giving the jury who served on the case a say on the sentencing as well as the verdict. For example, if a jury found a man guilty of GBH I would then invite them to give their assessment of what they thought to be a fair punishment. Prosecution and defence lawyers would have the opportunity to make their representations to judge and jury, who would weigh up both sides and reach a decision on what the sentence should be, in a fair and open way. This would at least guarantee a say for the Man in the Street who in my opinion is in the best position to decide what justice means because he's out there dealing with the consequences of crime on a daily basis. As it is, everything is controlled by solicitors, barristers and judges with lifestyles so privileged they're out of touch with the society they're supposed to represent.

As for the punishments available to courts, I have to say that although I generally favour harsher penalties, I don't believe that locking someone up and throwing away the key is the only answer. I like the idea of community service – if someone is convicted of graffiti or causing damage to public property then they should be the one responsible for putting it right. I'd support moves to make anyone convicted of vandalism clear up ten times the mess they made – minimum. Graffiti one wall? Clean ten. Cause damage to one school? Be made to visit ten more and help with whatever repair work needs doing.

Follow the American model, put them in orange boiler suits and sentence them to proper hard labour on their community's behalf. It's the least they can do. If the sweat and toil of back-breaking graft is not enough of a deterrent to keep them on the straight and narrow, maybe the humiliation of being seen by their mates in their new get-up will be. From 'cool' thug about town to idiot in a jump suit – maybe we can shame repeat offenders into behaving like respectful human beings.

I also like the idea of restorative justice, where the victim's feelings are taken into consideration and where the criminal is forced to understand the full impact of what they've done. Seeing at first hand the effect they have had on another human being is meant to help prevent them from inflicting the same pain in future, and this makes sense to me. I know that approach won't work for everyone because some people really just don't give a damn, but it is something we've tried on the show and I know it can be very effective.

Murderers, rapists and other dangerous criminals being seen to somehow get away with violent crime is surely one of the biggest threats to our society. I'm sorry, but if prison space is cramped and we have to make a choice between locking up a knife-wielding maniac or some boring tax evader, I'd go with Stabby McPsycho every time. We need to know that serious and violent crimes are going to be properly punished, and that means getting criminals off the streets, away from their family and friends and serving some hard jail time.

I am told that the more criminals get off lightly, the more serious their crimes become. It makes sense that when justice hasn't happened and there haven't been any consequences for their actions, they think they can get away with even more the next time. Often, in murder or manslaughter trials the offender has more than fifty previous convictions. As they escape more or less scot-free time and again – perhaps with a small fine or an ASBO they can brag to their mates about – they get bolder and more vicious.

Too many families I see have to suffer the double blow of having a crime committed against them then reliving the full horror of it in a court of law, only to see the grinning thug responsible for their pain waved out of court to carry on as before. This must stop.

I just think that some of our judges and law lords are out of touch with public opinion – criminals getting away with it is a subject that deeply upsets millions of people, shouldn't that be taken into account? The problem is that our legal system is too susceptible to being manipulated by those clever men in wigs – you can bend it one way or the other so long as you can afford the right lawyer. Everyone knows it and everyone can see it – too often, justice is not being done and the entire system seems to be weighted on the side of the criminal.

I want what every decent human being up and down this land wants – a properly fair criminal justice system. If there are too many easily exploitable loopholes, let's close them. If the judges are the problem, let them make way for people better qualified to represent society. Build in the voice of Everyman and let the people, by way of the jury, have their say on sentencing. And if all else fails they can always ask my dad ... I have thought for a very long time now that someone like my dad would make a perfect judge. He's no legal eagle but he's got a moral compass made of solid gold. If he were given the position of, say, a Sentencing Consultant, in a court, I know he would do what is right. My dad and so many like him – fair-minded, upstanding, senior citizens whose guiding force in life has been to work hard, try to do the right thing and ensure their families do the same – would be perfect to advise on cases in this way. As a country we're blessed with millions of honest and community-minded citizens – teachers, doctors, police would be a good place to start – and we should be making the most of them. If people are fed up with listening to me, then I say listen to my dad – he'd be perfect for this!

33

I'm a Celebrity (with a DVD to sell) – Get Some People in Here!

Not so long ago I was astonished to read in a newspaper that while he was promoting his autobiography, Chris Evans, media mogul, nineties legend and all-round broadcasting genius, was left stranded alone in a bookshop, not a single fan in sight. To anyone who can remember just how big he was only a few years back that seems faintly ridiculous. To me it was downright unbelievable. He was *the* celebrity of that decade. He made millions from his brilliance and had a life that was the envy of everyone who was hooked on his shows. *The Big Breakfast, Don't Forget Your Toothbrush* and *TFI Friday* were must-see TV. His Radio 1 *Breakfast Show* rescued the station by making it relevant again. He expertly wielded both the Midas and the common touch, achieved almost unimaginable success and even managed to make being ginger and specky cool! Well, that might be going too far, but he certainly made them work for him. And say what you like about him and his excesses, he always was and still is brilliant.

I found it so weird to read that just twenty-six people

(eventually) showed up to his recent book signing in Manchester. And apparently the first guy in the queue was only there because he mistakenly believed the author was Chris Moyles. Ouch. Insult, meet Injury, how do you do?

I reasoned that this poor turnout must be down to the fact that he was no longer regularly on telly. Now that his face wasn't on screen every day, people had just forgotten about him and moved on. It happens in showbiz. A lot. I figured that selling my show's *Access All Areas* DVD to the people of Great Britain would be a doddle. Last year I was on TV a whopping 1063 times. ITV1, ITV2, ITV2+1 – I'm bloody everywhere, you can't get away from me! My show pulls in about two million viewers every day so I reckoned I would be bombproof against the sort of humiliation poor Chris Evans suffered in Manchester. With that many people watching, surely I'd be all right.

Everyone else was confident, too. All the people at ITV kept telling me that in the run-up to Christmas the chance to get their hands on our £12.99 stocking filler would be irresistible for an audience as loyal as ours . . . ITV thought they were on to surefire winner, but that's not quite how things turned out.

Picture the scene. I am sat alone, just like Chris Evans, waiting for the hordes to flock to the store, all clutching their copy of the DVD I was getting ready to gratefully sign. However, where Chris Evans was warmed and welcomed – albeit by fewer people than he would have liked – I was ordered to freeze in a supermarket in Sheffield. Almost literally as it turns out. I was tucked away, hidden apologetically like some dirty secret between two great, growling freezers. Anyone casually browsing the aisles that day would have had an unusual selection of products to choose from: frozen veg, frozen chips, Jeremy Kyle, frozen turkeys, ice cream.

There was no sign of the hundreds of happy viewers I'd been promised. Nope, humble pie was served in barely two dozen portions that day. Any notions I might have had that I was a big star or a famous face were dispelled immediately. My Evans-inspired theory about TV exposure lay in tatters. About twenty people turned up and I'm sure half of them were coaxed into the store at the last minute with promises of a two-minute trolley dash. I half suspected the manager might just lock the doors and have the cleaners herd everyone towards me with their mops. I was waiting for the tannoy to crackle to life with an announcement. 'No one is allowed to leave until this insignificant celebrity feels just a little bit better about himself, OK? Oh, and there's 20p off free range eggs if anyone's interested!'

Anyway, some people are better than no people. This project was important to both me and ITV, and it was the least I could do to smile sweetly and sign the DVDs of the people who had shown up. I may have been disappointed but that wasn't their fault. They had made the effort and so I resolved to take more time than I normally can and really make a fuss of those brave few in the queue. I would make the best of it, have a bit of a chat, pose for photos and write proper long messages on the newly bought copies of my DVD. But hold on a minute, the first five people were all clutching copies of my first book! I obliged, signed and thanked them anyway but as the people continued to pass, I saw no sign of the new DVD. Midway through, at about the fifteen mark, came a woman who had nothing at all for me to autograph. She just wanted to see who I was and what I was doing sat in front of the Christmas turkeys. Given how the day was unfolding, it was probably the best place for me.

After a few more people, this time with neither book nor DVD, I couldn't help myself, I had to ask, 'Can I interest anyone in a Jeremy Kyle DVD to go with their Findus Crispy Pancakes?' I felt like I'd gone back twenty years and was a salesman all over again, but hey, I had to do my best. I needn't have bothered. It took a kindly pensioner to put me out of my misery. This lovely lady waited until I'd finished, looked down at me with pity in her eyes and said, 'Jeremy, I'd love to buy a copy but look over there – they haven't got any of your DVDs.'

I looked to where she was pointing. It was true. I had driven 250 miles, four hours from home for a signing in a store with twenty-seven people, none of whom could have bought the DVD even if they had wanted to – because nobody had thought to order some copies and put them on the shelves! Brilliant!

My morning's misery was made complete when the final happy shopper of the day leaned in for her signing. No DVD, no book and not even any groceries to sign. No. This lady reached into her handbag, rooted around for a while and then proceeded to unfurl a crumpled piece of toilet paper I can only hope had not been used. Ripped off the roll back home, I presume she'd had in mind another use for it if ever she got caught short that day but hey, I was here, this was an opportunity and any old shit was clearly good enough for her four sheets of quilted two-ply.

My experience proved I was wrong about Chris Evans's

book sales figures. They rocketed regardless of him not being on TV so much nowadays. In fact, as I found out myself, even being on the box as much as I am is no guarantee of popularity or even mild interest in what you have to say or sell.

34

Criminal Stupidity

It surely won't come as any major surprise to learn that I tend to take a fairly hard line on Law and Order. Not the TV show – never watched it – but the everyday approach we adopt with regards to crime and punishment. Soft-touch sentences, as I've already said, are too commonplace and I am genuinely concerned about the fear of crime that grips too many who only want to be able to walk the streets without wondering if today's the day they might become the next statistic.

I find I have the least patience for those pathetic petty criminals who turn to stealing because they're too damn lazy or lacking in curiosity to give something (anything!) more challenging, like trying to find work, a go instead. Given my antipathy towards these louts it might seem a little misplaced to give any of them public acknowledgement here, but I'm sorry, I just can't help myself!

Now don't worry, I'm not about to thank a raft of little idiots who tried to turn criminal because they couldn't be bothered to be anything else. I won't do that, but with a wry smile, and probably a touch too much Schadenfreude, I will give thanks to the idiocy that drove them. For while I deplore the crimes they committed, and any pain they inflicted, I can't help laughing at how some of them came a cropper!

I admit I've had the odd bad day made a little better by reading how certain criminals have been caught out by nothing more than their own bungling incompetence. No need for Miss Marple and barely worth a call to PC Plod, these chaps did all the detective work on the cases against themselves *by* themselves, proving beyond any doubt that the age of the truly stupid criminal is now upon us.

I initially thought this emerging cultural phenomenon was a uniquely American quirk. Certainly, the first reports I read of this type came from the States. There were the two robbers who couldn't find suitable disguises and so went out for a mini burgling spree with nothing but hastily (and badly) scribbled marker pen on their faces! Not even a mask, a tea towel or stolen pair of tights. Marker pen! What were they thinking? They looked like they'd lost a fight with an Etch-a-sketch. You hardly look set for a hard-knock life of crime when your get-up is that of someone who's just been graffitied, like the first drunk person to fall asleep at a student party!

I also read about a couple of teenagers in California who were rumbled by police, trying to break into a parked car. Predictably they legged it and high-tailed it over a large fence at the end of the road. They left the chasing cops in their wake and scaled the fence with consummate, youthful ease. Unfortunately for them, when they dropped down the other side they realised that they were probably the first people in history ever to have broken *into* San Quentin prison!

As I say, I thought the curse of the (criminally) stupid criminal was something confined to American news reports.

As ever though, where they blaze a trail we inevitably follow and more recently I have noted that rank idiocy is alive and kicking in our criminal fraternity too. For example, there was the man in Scarborough who held up a shop disguised in a crash helmet. Good move, face obscured, sound plan, yes? No! The helmet he wore had his name emblazoned right across the front for all his victims to make a note of before the police arrived. If that is not bad enough, consider the case of Christopher Walker . . .

Christopher is the bright spark who on a whim decided to end a run of bad luck by robbing a bank. He overpowered a security guard with a stick and somehow managed to relieve Lloyds TSB of £25,000. So far, so good for our would-be Ronnie Biggs. Things got even better for him as he bundled up the cash and made a quick getaway, showing a clean pair of heels to a variety of witnesses who had no hope of keeping up with him. Christopher Walker made it all the way home and must have been feeling pretty pleased with himself until the inevitable knock came loud and true at his front door. Yes it was the police, yes they had their man and no, it hadn't taken them any time to find him. Why? Well, Christopher Walker had robbed his local bank! His house was right across the road, twenty-five yards away from the branch. The witnesses who'd seen him steal the money barely had to say anything to the arriving police. A simple point towards his front door with one hand as they tried to stifle a giggle with the other was all they had to do!

As the snow came down at the start of 2010, another beacon of brightness came up with the idea of stealing a car from a British street. This was down near my parents, in Taunton, Somerset. Evidently our enterprising young thief did not have much luck with his intended vehicle. Disturbed before breaking into it, he scarpered home. As with Mr Walker though, the police soon caught up with him. They had to travel more than the twenty-five yards it took to apprehend him but the process was made simple by the prevailing weather. The arresting officer must almost have been embarrassed to admit that 'yes, I caught him' by employing that little-known Secret Service tactic of following the tracks the culprit had made in about three feet of newly laid snow! How very OO7!

For the more discerning thief, of course, there is always the option of using a getaway driver. What better way to beat a hasty retreat from the scene of the crime? Another Brit, David Field, had this idea not so long back as he and some friends tried to help themselves to a few 'free' tellies from an Argos store in Holyhead, North Wales. The only problem was that none of them had brought their own car. Instead they tried booking a cab to help them escape! As they bundled into the back seat with armfuls of stolen goods, they looked, panicked, at the driver and David uttered the immortal word, 'Drive!' The cabbie's response was, 'Are you having a laugh?'

Unsurprisingly, all the people I have mentioned above were caught. How could they not be? They will have been processed through the justice system but how do we protect ourselves from these criminals in future? Moreover, how do we protect these criminals from themselves? It is probably unfair to heap further punishment on people who are still reeling from the bum deal they got in the gene pool. Nevertheless, perhaps more jail time is the answer, just a little longer to get the message through? Maybe we should stick another couple of years on the sentence of anyone who compounds their crimes by attempting to execute them with appalling stupidity. Call it a stupidity tax. That said, we would have to ensure that we didn't send them to Kirkham's Category D prison in Lancashire. This was the jail that proved that the criminal stupidity bug was contagious, and spreading from convicts to wardens. Something clearly affected the governors there, how else could they sanction a raffle where inmates paid one pound per head for the chance to win a day's freedom?!

With this lunacy in mind, perhaps it would be best if the truly criminally stupid were spared prison altogether. We could maybe invite them to talk at high schools instead. They could tour the country explaining to morning assemblies what they did and precisely how they got caught. Just imagine the response they would get from a mob of merciless teens. That would be all the penance society ever needed them to pay and it might just prove a deterrent, ramming the message home to even the most intellectually challenged of criminals, not to be so silly again!

35

An Englishman in New York

We've all faced phone calls we were scared of making. We've all had others where we couldn't wait to get dialling. We've all swerved calls from certain people at certain times just as at others we've sat there staring at our phone, willing that special someone to ring. I have an agent and as all of my work and earnings have to flow through him before they get to me, I have to answer the phone whenever he calls. And that brings a problem.

An agent rarely calls to talk about the weather. I have been with my agent, Grant, over eight years now and we are way past the 'getting to know' phase that is so crucial at the start, when that professional relationship is first being built. Grant and I have become firm friends and as such there is no need for him to check in with me every ten minutes to find out what I had for breakfast or see what I watched on TV last night. No, Grant only calls me now to deliver good news or bad. Actually, in this industry, it's more like brilliant or awful. There's rarely any in between, so it's hard not to get a bit jumpy whenever I see his number come up for an unscheduled call.

For example, Grant's number flashes up whenever my

show or my past has been dragged through the press. I detailed in my last book just what a devastating effect the news that you are to be the news can have on a person who has never experienced it before. When I was first told that some highly embarrassing stories about me were going to be splashed across the *News of the World*, I fell to pieces. I couldn't bear the thought of my family and everyone else reading all the gory details the paper was promising to print. That whole horrible period in my life started with a phone call from my agent. Back then, any time 'Grant' lit up my ringing phone I just wanted to hide or be sick or both. At other times that same name and that same number has precipitated some of the most euphoric phone calls I have ever had, ones that left me stunned, elated and speechless when I finally hung up. It's a weird sort of electricity that shoots through me whenever I see that Grant's calling. I know I have to answer the call but I am always fifty-fifty as to whether he's about to make my day or ruin my week.

Grant has called through with the best of news, the worst of news and sometimes just the most bizarre. Back in 2009 he told me that Covonia – the cough syrup Ainsley Harriet yodels about every time I turn on the telly – had been in touch. Not for work on their next voiceover, alas, but because they had shortlisted me for an award! Apart from something for a radio show I broadcast about thirteen years ago, I've never won any award. My excitement at this one was short-lived though – they basically wanted to honour me as something tantamount to their Gobshite of the Year! Cheers.

It was also Grant who called to tell me I'd come second in a poll for some of the world's most memorable men. Sadly we were memorable for all the wrong reasons and I was actually runner up in the race for the prize every young boy dreams about telling their mum they've won, World's Most Hated Man! Yup, as I think I mentioned before, I do keep some illustrious company! The final placings were: Fifth – Adolf Hitler. Fourth – Pol Pot. Third – Saddam Hussein. Second – ME! And in first place: OSAMA BIN LADEN! That's quite something for a mere talk show host! My parents must be so proud. Before getting back to work after that call, Grant gleefully mocked my continuing losing streak. 'Most Hated Man in the World and you couldn't even win that,' he laughed down the line as he clicked off. Ha bloody ha, thanks very much!

Without doubt the best call my agent has ever made to me was the one which confirmed that this little boy from Coley Park, Reading was actually going to get a crack at working in America. Yep, the United States! By the time this book is launched I should be getting ready to fly across the Atlantic to have a shot at building my very own American dream. Few people outside the industry will grasp just how exciting this move could be for me and my family. We've all read about various Brits trying to 'break' America – Oasis, Robbie Williams, Ant 'n' Dec have all had a go and so have so many more. However, it is never really explained why. Essentially, as the song goes, if you make it there, you can make it anywhere and for me, a chance at making it in America is the stuff of pure fantasy. The riches and rewards on offer if it goes well out there are out of this world. I think I'm living in a dreamland in the UK at the moment, but to do what I do here, there, would be to live the dream that only my dreams have dared dream of.

Financial security apart there is also the newness and the

adventure of it all. My young family are hugely excited at us packing our bags and trying to find our fortune on foreign shores. The kids don't entirely get it but the chance of what would feel like an extended summer holiday for them in an amazing, exciting place is right up their street. For me to work in the home of talk shows, to learn from the best of the best - that is just amazing too. The whole project is fraught with risk and I know nothing will be gained without a whole heap of hard work, but just to have the chance to have a crack at the American Dream that is the stuff of showbiz legend is more than anything I could have dared hope for right up to even a few years ago.

The process all started about two years ago with a few phone calls between an American network and my agent. There was a period of professional flirting that went on a while and I was only dimly aware of things happening in the background. Apparently kind words were spoken about me in some very pleasant transatlantic phone calls to Grant. He took some advice and with the blessing of our then boss at ITV, he reciprocated and no doubt started to try and be a bit more charming than his usual self. I guess the whole process was a bit like two teenagers circling each other at the school disco, desperate to dance but too scared to make the first move. Grant kept me informed as the months drifted by but it didn't start feeling real until we were finally invited out to a meeting in New York.

Wow, how exciting was this! They sorted everything. They laid it all on and treated us like proper stars! I had to keep checking it was me they wanted to see. Jeremy Kyle? The motormouth from England, right? Yes? Really? OK then, bring it on . . . Business class on the plane. Stretch-limo to pick us up from the airport and a few hours to kill in Manhattan before the biggest meeting of my life!

Before such a big event in both our lives you might have thought that my agent would take me off somewhere quiet and coach and prepare me, like a trainer would a boxer before going for the heavyweight title. Get to a hotel, get your client relaxed and ready for the fight of his life, right? Well no – not with my agent.

Always a man to spot when the percentages are going his way, Grant used our down time before the meeting to drag me to the shops. He'd spotted that Abercrombie & Fitch had a half-price sale on and reckoned this was a (shop) window of opportunity to stock up on clothes for the kids for the next four years.

For three bloody hours he dragged me around that store until I finally snapped and urged him to get his head back to matters more pressing than family fashion. He relented and agreed that we could go for a latte next door. We supped coffee and finally re-focused on the forthcoming 'meeting of our lives', before going back to the hotel to get changed. It was only once back in our room that Grant confessed he'd left all his shopping back in the café!

With no time to apply the deodorant I needed to disguise my nerves, I was dragged back out onto the streets of New York, trailing behind my agent like a toddler hanging on to a parent rushing for a train. Far from going into a Zen-like state of calm, I prepared for what I'd decided would be an *Apprentice*-style American grilling by running myself ragged in search of Grant's mountain of discounted denim. Needless to say I was in a bit of a mess when we finally pitched up, and more than a little sweaty!

The meeting took place in the Rockefeller Center, the place where they have the huge Christmas tree everyone ice skates around in all the films. I kept pinching myself as I sat there talking to a few of the most impossibly powerful figures in the American TV industry. It seemed to be a nice, knock-about chat and everyone was so polite and charming I had to keep reminding myself just what might be at stake.

It lasted a couple of hours. They said they liked me and hoped the sort of show I did in the UK could also work for them in the US. The feeling was mutual. I liked them – a lot – and what I wanted more than anything else in the world at that time was to show that it definitely could work in the US. I wanted to prove them right and so many others wrong – I wanted a shot at breaking America. We shook hands, agreed to talk further and as I took one of those famous yellow cabs back to the airport it felt like I was floating in some sort of dream. Could this really be happening? And to me of all people?

No! It couldn't. Not then anyway. I should have got some sense of how the fates were stacking up against me the minute I landed back on English soil. That night I flew back into what felt like a war zone. Rangers fans had taken over the whole of Manchester city centre for the UEFA Cup Final and there were running battles going on everywhere I looked. The streets ran a little with blood and a lot with urine that must have been almost flammable if the amount of empty whiskey bottles being smashed all around was anything to go by! I spoke to my then boss the next day, and she could see I was excited, but she explained that she had known too many of these deals to go up in smoke before, and so we were to keep calm – and schtum – for now.

She was right. The recession hit. Big time. That meant the money to strike new deals dried up and in the US there was none left in the pot to take any punts on unknown faces from across the Pond. For a time I felt deflated but I understood. The recession was having a big impact on everyone and as I saw for myself at ITV, cutbacks were being made here, there and everywhere. In Manchester we all twitched nervously as job losses were announced. Leeds felt the axe first and then I read reports that my show was to go too! There was an air of angst and depression that dogged all of my colleagues whenever I was up there for work. Grant hadn't called though so there was no real bad news to contend with yet. Equally though, no calls from him meant no positive news from the States either. My American dream had been put so far back on the back burner that it was just pie in the sky once more. Of greater concern now was the show and team I was a part of back home in Blighty.

Despite plenty of rumours to the contrary it survived. Just. Half of my office was made redundant and production was scaled right back from the levels of previous years. Pay cuts were the order of the day for most people working in front of the camera at ITV and I had to take my medicine too. I had to wave goodbye to many of the friends I had made in Manchester as the reality of job losses finally lapped up at our shores, and I honestly thought I'd be next. My contract was running down to the point where there were only a couple of months left on it. I thought if they really wanted me they would have said so sooner. Football clubs extend their best players' contracts long before their end dates to keep them out of their competitors' clutches but mine was being run down to the wire. I got it into my head that they were probably avoiding me until that last day when they would have to tell me, 'Sorry, we're not renewing. Have a nice life!' At this time the intermittent conversations with America took on a whole new light. They still seemed keen and although it was still a remote possibility, I started to wonder if they might be the only people interested in employing me!

This whole period lasted about eighteen months. It was a thumbs-up from everyone but the money men in America, but back over here it was a case of 'we just don't know.' Thankfully the cull that turned our show's Manchester base into a ghost town stopped before it took us all down. The show and half of the office had survived and we signed a deal to keep filming in the UK through 2011. Phew! Panic over and feeling wanted again, I resolved to get my head down, work hard and hope that the bad times affecting everyone would pass soon. But then, out of the blue, new life was suddenly breathed into my American dream and the people resuscitating it were ITV! There were some new people in charge and they were as excited by the possibility as I was.

Within a couple of months of to-ing and fro-ing they proved as good as their word. Soon enough I got that phone call I'd always dreamed of from Grant, the one telling me that he'd crossed all the t's, dotted the i's on the prospective contract that would take us to the U S of A. He finished by telling me that all I had to do was sign it. Now good vibes don't come much better than that, let me tell you. I was ecstatic!

The contract itself arrived a couple of weeks later. It was delivered by hand to my table as I ate breakfast in the hotel in Manchester with my good friend Kiernan, the man who has been charged with the unenviable task of making this book readable. I tried to take it all in but couldn't really. The words were a blur and so I had to just trust that my lawyer had done his job properly. I could have been signing up to appear naked at the local circus for all I knew. And then it hit me. After two years of hoping, dreaming and then wondering if it was just not meant to be, I suddenly felt a bit drained, exhausted even. I gave the contract my squiggle whilst still in a daze and I think I may even have spilt some coffee on it as I handed it back. I can't quite remember, all I knew was that it was now done. I was going to America!

And here we are. I have been signed up to see if American networks and viewers might take to what we do. Who knows if they will? I might end up doing one show, two shows or two thousand shows out there but to be able to say I got hired for even one really does mean the world. After five years in the UK, ITV have teamed up with Debmar Mercury and I am to go to New York in 2011 to film a batch of shows which will hopefully air all over America pretty soon thereafter. If it goes well, the hope is to return and do more.

Since the news was announced a lot of people have asked if I think it will work or if American audiences might like me. Of course I very much hope it does work. I'd love to live the dream of working in the UK for half the year and in the US for the other but that isn't a decision I'll get to make. I can't say if people in America will like what we do, all I know is that I will work hard to learn what I can from the American producers and crew whilst remaining true to myself.

America is well used to the talk show format I present. In

fact they are traditionally streets ahead of the UK when it comes to producing shows of that type. As much as anything I am hoping to learn out there and apply what I can to make our show back here even stronger too. In the US I've seen some where presenters throw chairs at their guests, or have police waiting to arrest the paedophiles they've been interviewing live on stage. People think I go too far over here but I am tame in comparison. And if tame is how I'm viewed out there, so be it. I'll think the same, talk the same and react the same way to situations wherever I am on the planet so I can't see me changing what I do over here, just because I'm doing it over there. It would feel wrong and it would be wrong.

No. I will bring what I can, do what I can and work as hard as I can but everything I get to do in the US will have to be underpinned by the same values and ethos we bring to shows in the UK. Most of all, I want to bring the aftercare we do in the UK to the US and see if our approach can get the same great results on both sides of the Atlantic. I have always known I am nothing without the teams working behind me and as far as *The Jeremy Kyle Show* goes there is no team more important than Graham's aftercare team. Long may that be the case, wherever we are in the world.

And so, the next chapter of my life is about to begin just as the last chapter of this book is coming to a close. These are potentially exciting times. Scary ones, yes, but ones filled with such promise too. I really do feel like I am entering a new phase of my life, one where I feel more confident, more comfortable and more positive. I have one child who's flown the nest to make a life on the other side of the world, and now I'm hoping I can take a leaf out of that daughter's book and do the same. The other kids are too young to take in the enormity of what might lie in wait for us with a transatlantic move but they are up for it nonetheless. Little Henry will bounce onto whatever plane and smile his way through from take-off to landing. Alice will sing and dance and grab her own American adventure with open arms. Ava probably couldn't care less one way or the other but Carla and I know that come what may, this is one of those experiences we'll look back on in our old age, and probably pinch ourselves to ask if it really happened at all.

It seems like a dream already, it's like you couldn't make it up!

ACKNOWLEDGEMENTS

It is never lost on me that I would not be where I am today, and certainly not enjoying the wonderful opportunities that come my way, were it not for the help and unflinching support of so many around me . . .

Fenella, it really has been the greatest pleasure working alongside you on this book. Thank you for your dedication to the cause, all of your input and thanks also to the whole team at Hodder.

Grant, my agent and great friend: a man who has helped plan and manage the greatest years of my life, and what promises to be the journey of a lifetime.

Graham, for your loyalty and unswerving friendship, in times good and bad. Thank you for having my back, always. It is ALWAYS appreciated.

Lou, for your unparalleled expertise and the ball-breaking efficiency with which you wield it, thank you.

Amir, your patience, your loyalty and your professionalism are all second to none but they are nothing compared to the friendship and first-rate advice you provide, day by day, mile after mile. Thank you so much. For everything.

Nadine – for the ever-generous loan of your husband, thank

you. And good luck when 'The Dark Lord' arrives. You're blooming now and you'll be bloomin' marvellous when Finlay's finally here.

Kiernan, I've not cracked you yet but I'm getting there. Clearly you've 'got' me though, and in more ways than you realise. Thank you for all the blood, sweat and tears continually invested on my behalf.

To the whole team at ITV. This book and these opportunities would not come were it not first and foremost for all the hours you slavishly devote each and every day to making *The Jeremy Kyle Show* the success it has become. Thank you all.

And finally to my wife, Carla. Thank you for putting up with me throughout this process, and always in fact.